Contents

Introduction

The significance of your birthday   04

What are annual profections?   06

The Twelve Astrological Houses:

The First House   16

The Second House   24

The Third House   32

The Fourth House   40

The Fifth House   48

The Sixth House   56

The Seventh House   64

The Eight House   72

The Ninth House   80

The Tenth House   88

The Eleventh House   96

The Twelfth House   104

The real *significance* of your *birthday*

In the astrological world, birthdays are one of the most important anchor points of your year. They are referred to as your Solar Return as this is when the Sun (solar) is returning to exactly the same spot it was when you were born.

WHILE WE KNOW that the Earth orbits the Sun scientifically, astrology views the sky from our Earth-based perspective, making it appear as if the Sun is moving around us. This journey, known as the solar or tropical year, takes about a year and marks a complete cycle.

Like an adventurer returning home, your birthday signifies that you have reached the end of a year-long cycle and that a new, different adventure is about to start in your journey of life.

Over 2,000 years ago, classical astrologers had developed techniques that dived more deeply into the experience of each birth year. They understood that different parts of life would be activated in different years and placed this information within a 12-year cycle. This information was lost for hundreds of years, but was then retrieved 30 years ago so that many people now understand the importance of their birthday from a different perspective.

Rather than being a day solely to celebrate your birth, it is also a day which signifies the beginning of your very own new year. Unlike the collective New Year experience on the 1st January when nothing fundamentally changes, this isn't the case when it comes to your personalized new year.

When you enter a new age, you are entering into a completely different environment and as such your reactions and desires will be connected to this new landscape.

Ultimately there is something immensely personal about your birthday. Your birthday is a place between worlds – knowing that a new adventure is about to start, there is a sense that the person setting out at the beginning of the year will be quite different to the one returning home.

My hope is that this book becomes a treasured keepsake that you will return to time and time again. Decades after I first opened the doors to the astrological world, it continues to be a steadfast source of wisdom and guidance, helping me understand myself and my experience of the ever-changing world around me. My wish is that you, too, find support from this book and a sense of connection to something greater than you could possibly imagine.

Prompt

Reflect on your year gone by before you look forward, towards the new horizon.

What are annual *profections?*

The style of 'Modern astrology' is focused on how the planets influence you from a psychological perspective and came to prominence at the turn of the 20th century.

MY FORMAL TRAINING and personal exploration of the astrological world has been aligned to modern astrology, which differs from 'traditional astrology' which dates back to ancient Mesopotamia and is more oriented towards external events.

While these approaches are different, there are many incredible tools that have been rediscovered from these ancient times especially when it comes to forecasting and timing techniques.

Chris Brennan, author of *Hellenistic Astrology* is an expert on the astrology that was practiced in the Mediterranean region between the first century BCE and the seventh century. It is through his detailed analysis that I first started to utilize these 'time lord' techniques, many of which date back over 2,000 years.

One of these hoary tools that I value the most is called annual profections. Originating from Hellenistic astrology, the term 'profection' comes from the Latin word *profectio* meaning 'progression' or 'moving forward'.

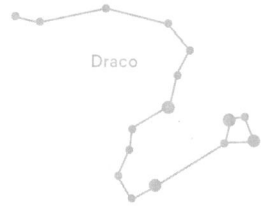

Draco

This ancient practice was used to predict life events and themes based on your age.

This technique is straightforward and in its simplest form doesn't require you to have any previous astrological knowledge. I always include this insight when working with a client as it immediately sets the scene and shows me which chapter of my client's life is being activated.

To use annual profections you need to be aware of two concepts. The first one is that there are 12 astrological houses. Each house describes an environment which relates to specific areas of your life.

The second concept is that each year of your life is mapped onto one of these 12 astrological houses. This means that on your birthday, you move into a new astrological house. You remain in this house for the whole year and then move on to the next house on your next birthday.

Cassiopea

Where *are you* on the cycle?

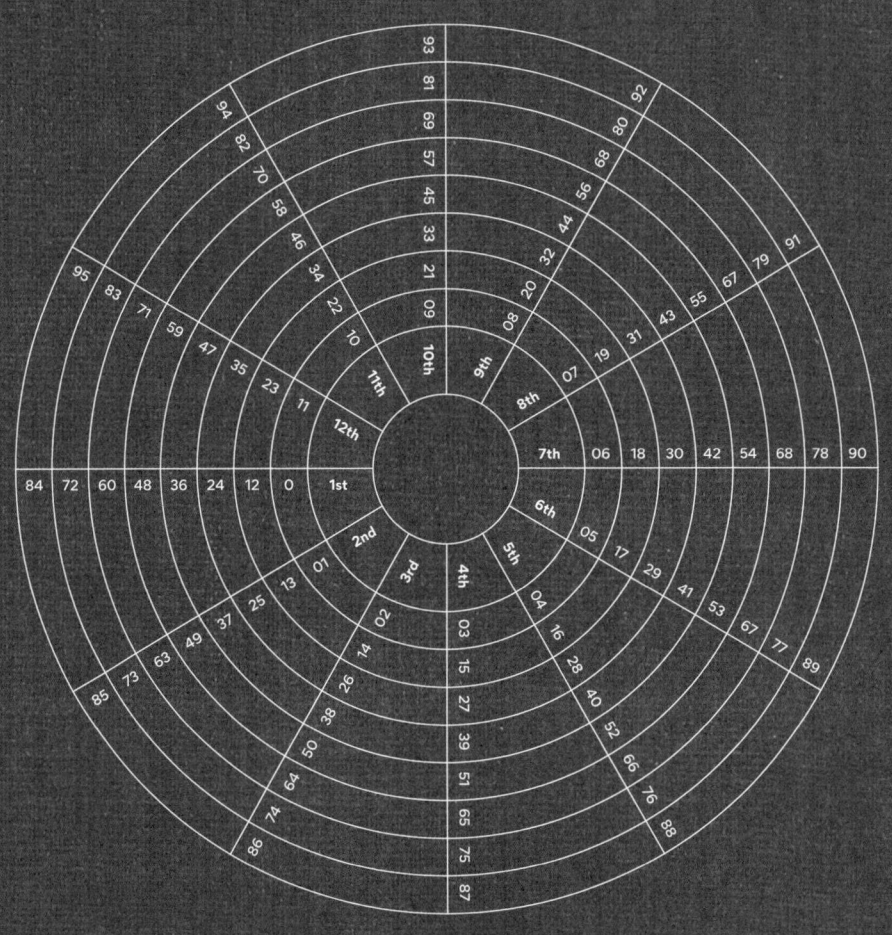

Natal Chart

ON THE OPPOSITE page, you will see the annual profections cycle. This essentially is a wheel divided into 12 sections. If you look at the inner core of the wheel you will see that each house is labelled. Start at the first house (positioned halfway down on the left-hand side) – you can see that the cycle moves in an anticlockwise motion and finishes at the 12th house.

You'll also notice that there are eight circles mapped on top of each house. These circles represent each year of your life. If we start at the beginning, when you were born, you started life in the 1st house. If you look at the segment above the 1st house you'll see the numeral 0 – this means zero years, the age you were before your first birthday.

When you are born, you start in the 1st house; on your first birthday, you move into the second house and you'll see the number '01' positioned above the 2nd house – this represents your life at one year old. When you are two years old you'll move into the 3rd house and when you are three years old you'll move into the 4th house, this continues around the wheel as you grow up.

When you are 12 years old, you re-enter the 1st house as you have completed a 12-year cycle. So, say you are 47 years old, you can see that this year belongs to the 12th house domain. The wheel also shows that you were last here when you were 35 years old and, before that, when you were 23. You first explored this territory when you were 11 years old.

This book is organized around the 12 astrological houses and offers a structured exploration of their significance. It's useful to recognize that each year is part of a larger 12-year cycle which highlights that certain years of your life are marked by important beginnings and endings.

Looking for *patterns*

TO MAKE THE MOST of annual profections it is useful to keep a record of the main events that occur in your life and if you can, revisit your past and make a note of the years that particularly stand out. This will help deepen your understanding of each house as through your records you'll start to notice stories that emerge and themes that repeat.

Examples of your own experiences may include:

* Major decisions such as changing career paths, making significant purchases or embarking on major life journeys.
* Beginnings or endings of relationships – whether romantic, friendship or professional.
* Promotions, career changes, starting a new business or taking on significant projects.
* Changes in financial circumstances such as substantial gains or losses or unexpected expenses.
* Educational achievements such as completing a degree, starting a new course or reaching significant learning milestones.
* Health issues, ranging from serious illnesses to major recoveries or lifestyle changes.
* Relocations, whether moving to a new home, city or country.
* Family-related events including births, deaths, marriages or divorces as well as miscommunications or reconciliations.

When you re-enter a house, you may notice echoes emerge that were connected to your last visit; this is because issues that were important then, often show up in a different form. This doesn't mean that if you experience an 'annus horribilis' that this is set to re-play on a 12-year loop. However, if you do experience a challenging year it can be helpful to step back and look at the situation in a bigger context. Understanding the house that is activated is always the first place to start and whether there are issues that have been left undone; proactively addressing often uncomfortable situations can hugely help alleviate potential problems that could arise the next time you revisit that particular house.

Advanced knowledge on annual profections

Annual profections offer invaluable insights regardless of your astrological experience. If you have access and understand your natal chart (downloadable from pruenichols.com) you can gain a more detailed perspective on your year ahead which would include the following:

1. Identifying the lord of your year:

Each house in your natal chart is ruled by a specific sign and each sign has a ruling planet. When you enter a house, the ruling planet becomes the 'lord of your year' making its transits and aspects particularly significant. For example, if you are entering the seventh house and you have Libra on the cusp of your seventh house, Venus (which rules Libra) will be your 'lord of the year.' Therefore Venus's movements, such as changing signs or going retrograde, will have a considerable impact on you.

2. Identifying activated planets:

Any natal planets that are located in the house that you are travelling through will have a heightened influence. For instance, if you are entering your tenth house and you have Mars positioned there, Mars will be activated. How this is expressed will be dependent on the sign that your natal Mars is in and the aspects it is making; however, it is likely that the Martian force will be a prominent feature of your year.

3. Integration with other astrological tools:

Annual profections provide a focused overview of what to expect for your year ahead. This knowledge and wisdom can be enhanced when integrated with other astrological tools such as secondary progressions and solar returns.

If you wish to go deeper with your astrological learnings, then you can book your own one-on-one session with me.

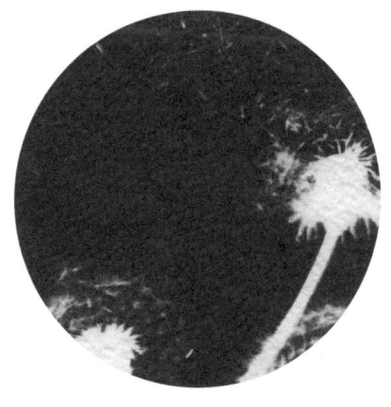

Introduction

How to *use* annual profections

THIS BOOK IS divided into the 12 houses so that you can explore whichever house you are in currently, or the house that you are about to enter on your next birthday. Each chapter is divided into specific segments which I have outlined below. Use this as a guide, incorporating the aspects that resonate with you and setting aside those that do not.

Elements In astrology, the four elements – **Fire, Earth, Air and Water** – play a crucial role in shaping the energy of each astrological house:

Fire Houses 1st, 5th, 9th
The fire element is activated when you move into these houses. As fire is associated with dynamic and initiating energy, you are likely to find it easier to take action, start new ventures and take a creative approach to your year.

Earth Houses 2nd, 6th, 10th
The earth element brings grounding energy to your year. These houses emphasize stability, practicality and material concerns, helping you focus on building a solid foundation and addressing practical matters.

Air Houses 3rd, 7th, 11th
As the air element is connected to intellectual and communicative qualities, these houses enhance your social interactions, support the exchange of ideas and encourage intellectual pursuits.

Water Houses 4th, 8th, 12th
The water element deepens emotional and intuitive experiences. These houses enhance emotional connections and foster introspective moments, allowing you to explore your inner world and strengthen emotional bonds.

House placement

Working out which house you are currently in is the first place to start. Unless you're 12 or younger, it won't be the first time that you experience this astrological terrain so reflecting on the years that you previously entered this house can provide useful information and valuable insights.

Keywords

This section lists three or four words that capture the core qualities of the house. Think of these as the main themes or spirit of the house. They provide a snapshot of the energy that you can expect, helping you to make sense of its most influential aspects.

Mantras

Mantras are powerful words or phrases repeated to aid in meditation, help focus the mind and evoke positive energy. They originate from ancient spiritual traditions and are used to promote mental clarity, emotional balance and spiritual growth. I have included mantras in this book to help you connect more deeply with the core qualities of each astrological house.

House environment

While each person will experience their house uniquely, the house environment section offers a guide on the key characteristics and themes of your house. The following section on entering the specific year goes into deeper exploration of what may arise, helping you to anticipate and prepare for upcoming experiences.

House support

The house support section offers practical advice and resources to support your year and make the most of the energies being stirred.

Journal prompts

Each chapter includes five journal prompts designed to help you explore your thoughts and feelings. Making notes will allow whatever needs you have to surface naturally. Set aside dedicated time for reflection in a quiet space where you can write freely. Consider using a new journal for each year to create a meaningful record of your personal growth and experiences.

Activities & practices

The activities are aligned with the energy of each house; these will provide practical ways to engage with and embody the unique lessons of each year. By participating in these activities, you can deepen your connection to the themes specific to your house.

Meditations

I have included a guided meditation for each of the 12 houses. You might wish to simply read these, or you can listen to them.

* Each meditation begins with you standing in the middle of a large circle surrounded by 12 doors. This circle represents your own natal chart and each door is an entry point to one of the 12 different astrological houses.

* A specific crystal type is suggested as an aid for each meditation. If you choose to use one, trust your intuition to decide where to place it – this could be on your third eye (or other chakra point), underneath a part of your body or simply in your hand.

* The type of essential oil is also recommended to enhance your experience. You can use essential oils in various ways, such as in a diffuser, on a tissue or by placing a drop on specific points on your body.

Before you begin the meditations, I have included a guided relaxation exercise here. Following this exercise before you start each meditation will ensure that you are able to make the most of your time as mental distractions will be released, enhancing your ability to move more deeply into mysteries of the unseen world.

Relaxation exercise

We are going to start by taking three deep breaths. With each breath, allow yourself to feel as if you are sinking deeper into your body, as if there is a magnetic gravitational pull re-earthing and reconnecting you to your physical home. Through your precious breath, let your whole being rest, giving permission for any discomfort, tension or dis-ease to dissipate and leave your body.

Focus your breath on the crown of your head, then slowly work down your body. Pause at each area with the intention to send light and healing breath to your forehead, neck, throat, shoulders, arms, heart, diaphragm, stomach, pelvis, hips and legs. Allow any tension to dissolve, feeling a lightness and release as you continue down to your calves and feet. Imagine roots emerging from the soles of your feet, reconnecting you to the nurturing care of Mother Earth.

Listen to the
meditations here.

innerworkproject.com/
product/stars-aligned

The
12
Astrological
Houses

The First House

Ages

0 | 12 | 24 | 36 | 48 | 60 | 72 | 84

Keywords

Beginnings, early experiences,
appearance, identity

Element

Fire

Mantra

I embrace new beginnings with
confidence and celebrate my unique
identity to achieve my most cherished
dreams and heartfelt goals.

The First House environment

) ● (

THE FIRST HOUSE is all about you – your mindset, your identity and your physical presence. This placement is seen as the most potent and powerful position of all the 12 houses. Traditionally described as 'the helm', ancient astrologers saw the first house as the steering wheel, responsible for the direction that your life was taking as well as the personal associations connected with moving forward.

The first house is a 'fire' house. Themes connected to life and identity burn brightly in this environment and typically bring with them an initiating quality and a desire for action. As the home of your first breath, the theme of 'firsts' and new beginnings is strongly emphasized here. Closely tied with your actual birth – both the feelings surrounding it and the event itself – this house is particularly influenced by early childhood; birth is seen as responsible for how easily life is taken in as well as the unconscious expectations that surround new phases of life.

Sue Tompkins in *The Contemporary Astrologer's Handbook* describes the first house as being the lens through which life is viewed. If you wear blue glasses, you see life through a blue prism, but someone else wearing different coloured glasses would see things from an alternative perspective and so on. This is helpful when understanding this environment as the House of Identity is underpinned by how you perceive yourself and your immediate surroundings.

Physicality also plays a central role in the first house. As your front door or shop window, this is the part of yourself which you visibly show to others. It's what people see when you walk into a room and includes all parts of your physical appearance from your body shape, weight, how you move to the clothes that you have chosen to wear. While health is associated with the sixth house, vigour and vitality are also included in the first house as this is part of your body's natural vibration and reveals how easily you can access this energy.

Entering your First House year

Overview

WHEN YOU ENTER your first house year, you are beginning a new 12-year cycle. This is one of the most important things to remember as the essence of newness is a central part of the first house environment.

As this is the house of your Self Identity it is expected that there will be shifts in your mindset – both how you perceive yourself as well as your immediate surroundings.

How you view 'new beginnings' will be dependent on your lens of life; while some people embrace change and transition, for others it can be a time of heightened worry and anxiety. If you can, remember that this environment is part of your cycle of evolution and the more that you are able to embrace what wishes to emerge, the easier and more enjoyable your first house year will be.

Reflecting on previous first house visits can be incredibly useful – how you experienced life during those specific years can deepen your understanding of your first house environment. What new beginnings emerged the last time you entered the first house? Can you see how different your life is because of this?

House support

Therapy/Coaching: As the core theme of the first house is Self Identity, this is an ideal year to focus on what makes you uniquely you. Having support at the beginning of a 12-year cycle can be immensely helpful and as you look to your personal horizon, you can ensure that you are making choices which are in alignment with who you are, rather than being influenced by external expectations.

Rebirthing: As this is the House of Birth, any blocks to starting out are impossible to ignore this year. As your own birth was your very first beginning, any traumas that occurred can unconsciously show up when making life decisions. If you are feeling blocked and/or lacking motivation and confidence, then this technique would be useful to explore.

Personal stylist: As the first house represents your appearance, you may notice that as you evolve so does your appearance. During a first house year, changes are often made in the wardrobe so having time to explore your appearance, especially the clothes that you have previously chosen is a particularly worthwhile activity.

First House

Journal prompts

How do I perceive my Self Identity?
What aspects of myself am I most proud of?

What fears or doubts are holding me back from starting
something new? How can I overcome them?

How do I present myself to the world?
What first impressions do I think I make on others?

Reflect on a recent experience where I felt confident
and assertive. What contributed to these feelings?

Reflect on a recent change or new experience in my life.
How has this impacted my personal growth?

A First House Activity
Fire gazing

For centuries, the element of fire has been used in ancient rituals. As the first house is a fire house, you are going to invoke this sacred element to see beyond the confines of the physical world and gain insight and wisdom as you begin an important life cycle. You don't need any previous fire experience; stay open-minded and trust your intuition.

Time: 30 minutes
Tools: Tall candle (preferably beeswax), candle holder and candle lighter.

1. Preparation:
* Set yourself up in a comfortable area of your house where you won't be disturbed by everyday life.
* Darken the room and take some slow, deep breaths.
* Notice your mind and create distance between yourself and all the mental chatter.
* Repeat three times, 'I love who I am,' then either out loud or in your mind, ask for insight that will support you during your first house year.

2. Fire gazing:
* When you feel calm and grounded, light your candle.
* Soften your eyes, allowing your gaze to blur and direct your focus to the centre of the wick.
* Watch the colours and movements of the fire, staying connected to the flame with soft eyes.
* Stay relaxed yet alert, and notice what images begin to emerge from the candle. Allow yourself to observe, trusting that you will see images in alignment with your highest interest.

3. Completion:
* After a few minutes, when you feel ready, blow out the candle.
* Ask that this insight continues to ripple forward into your first house year with increased luck and abundance.

A First House Meditation
Journey through the door of self

Begin with the relaxation exercise on page 12.

Crystal: Red jasper
Essential oil: Frankincense

Imagine that you are standing in the centre of a large circle. Around you are 12 doors, each representing portals to the 12 astrological houses. Each door is unique, with different shapes, colours and textures. One door, marked with the number one, draws you in and you walk towards it.

As you stand before it, the guardian of the house emerges. This is your guide, overseeing all the activity in your first house. What do they look like? How comfortable do you feel with them? They unlock the door with a large key, and you step into your first house.

You find yourself in a spacious room with many windows. What can you see through the windows? What does the terrain of your first house look like? Are there any people or activities happening? In this room you notice a large, floor-length mirror with a distinctive frame. You stand before the mirror and see your reflection. As the image becomes hazy, you see an older version of yourself. This is your future self, 12 years from now. They step out of the mirror and greet you warmly.

They tell you that you are about to embark on a 12-year journey, a potent time to envision your future. Consider what you want to create and move towards in your life. Together, you look in the mirror and see visions of your future life. What are you doing? You see yourself being bold, brave and fulfilled. Your future self passes you a compass, inscribed with 'true self' pointing north. You hold it in your palm, feeling its cool, smooth edges and see the needle deflect to the north axis.

Your future self explains that taking action that aligns with your true self will always guide you best. They ask if you have any questions. Think about what you want to ask. It's time to leave the room and you say goodbye to your future self. They return to the mirror and you are alone again. You walk past the windows and back to the door marked number one, carrying your compass. The guardian of the house opens the door and you step back into the circle. The guardian locks the door behind you. When you are ready, take slow, deep breaths, returning to your body, your room and your current life.

❝❞

Taking action that aligns with your TRUE self will ALWAYS guide you best.

Your Future Self

The Second House

Ages

1 | 13 | 25 | 37 | 49 | 61 | 73 | 85

Keywords

Possessions, money, resources and values

Element

Earth

Mantra

I honour my self-worth and align my values to create prosperity and abundance in all areas of my life.

The Second House environment

IN ANCIENT ASTROLOGY, the second house was known as the Gate of Hades. Hades, now more commonly referred to as Pluto, ruled the Underworld, overseeing the hidden aspects of life and the wealth and riches that can be revealed by confronting your darkest demons.

Traditionally, the position of this house was considered less favourable than the first as it was associated with the shadowy and concealed aspects of existence. As this house governs your money, security and resources, true motivations can remain hidden as influences driving your pursuit of material and emotional security may not always be apparent.

For your ancestors, second house themes were likely to include cattle, land and food as these were the essentials needed for survival. While these types of resources, the so-called 'moveable properties', required to sustain life have changed over time, this house still strongly emphasizes 'possessions'. This especially pertains to the things you acquire to satisfy your desire for psychological safety.

Without doubt this is the house connected to money – how you earn it, how you spend it and how you save it. However, the second house also holds a deeper significance related to values, as your financial habits reveal what is truly important to you. This isn't solely about the things you wish to possess; on a deeper level, this house reflects how you value yourself. High self-worth typically corresponds to a stronger flow of money while lower self-worth can often result in reduced money flow.

> ❝❞
> When you create SPACE, you create POSSIBILITY.
> **Dr Maryska Taylor**

Entering your Second House year

Overview

THIS YEAR IS THE TIME for you to focus on the broader aspects of your finances, as themes related to your personal sense of wealth are likely to surface.

Since this house is connected to what makes you feel safe and secure, any blocks or limitations in this area will be impossible to ignore. You may find yourself considering more deeply how you earn money and what you spend it on. If there is tension in this area, you are likely to feel an unconscious push to address and remedy it. You may also find yourself reconsidering what you value. Items and people that were once highly desired may no longer 'fit', prompting a decluttering process where you clear out possessions and re-evaluate relationships that no longer reflect what is important to you.

It is always useful to reflect on previous years spent in your second house. While you may not remember specific years, consider what was happening with your family during those times, particularly events related to money. This reflection can help you understand how your own values and attitude towards money have been shaped.

House support

Financial review: Taking a deep dive into your finances is particularly powerful when you are travelling through your second house. Look closely at your income, expenses, savings and investments to see if they align with your ideals. Making adjustments to create more concordance will pave the way for greater stability and prosperity.

Decluttering: Decluttering is particularly useful during a second house year as it helps to connect your physical space with your personal values. By removing items that no longer represent who you are, you create room for new opportunities and allow a clearer sense of what truly matters to you to emerge.

Grounding yourself in nature: Taking regular walks in nature is beneficial when you are in the second house. As an earth house, this year is ideal for reflecting on your beliefs and sense of security. Connecting with nature's abundance will ground your energy and align your inner values with the world around you, allowing you to focus on what is most important to you.

Second House

Journal prompts

How do I feel about my current financial situation?
What changes would I like to make?

What beliefs about money did I inherit from my family?
How do they impact my financial choices today?

How do my personal values influence my
financial decisions and habits?

How does my relationship with money affect my overall
sense of self-worth and wellbeing?

What lessons about money and values have
I learned from my past experiences?

A Second House Activity
Life values map

The Second House relates to the practical realities of life – what you value, how you use your resources and where your energy is spent. As an Earth house, it's about grounding yourself in what truly matters. This activity helps you reflect on key areas of your life, seeing what is in alignment with your values and what needs adjusting.

Time: 30 minutes–1 hour
Tools: Large piece of paper, sticky notes in various colours, at least one other person.

1. Identify key areas:
Think about what occupies your life, including work, family, relationships, hobbies, self-care and other activities you spend your time on or think about. Write down each aspect on a separate sticky note.

2. Setup:
Place a sticky note in the centre of the paper to represent you. Arrange the other sticky notes around this central note as you currently experience them.

3. Observation:
Observe how you feel seeing these aspects laid out. If doing this activity with someone else, discuss the different aspects of your life.

4. Rearrangement:
While keeping the sticky note representing you at the centre, rearrange any notes that don't align with your values or how you want to experience your life. Add an arrow to each sticky note:
* **Arrow towards you:** you want to experience more of this.
* **Arrow away from you:** you want to experience less of this.
* **Straight line:** you are happy with its current position.

5. Visualization:
Once you have finished arranging the notes, close your eyes and imagine living this life of alignment, attending to and building upon the areas that are most important to you.

A Second House Meditation
Unblocking financial flow & abundance

Begin with the relaxation exercise on page 12.

Crystal: Citrine
Essential oil: Patchouli

You find yourself standing in the centre of a large circle. You see 12 doors surrounding you. Each door is different. You walk up to the second door, taking in its colour, style and shape. You knock three times. The door opens and you step into your second house.

You are outside in nature, in the middle of a forest. Take some time to consider your surroundings. How do you feel standing in your second house? You notice a trail in front of you and start to follow it, listening to the sounds of the forest all around you. The trail brings you to a clearing surrounded by steep banks. In the middle of this clearing is a deep pool of water.

This water represents your unconscious attitude and connection to money. Take some time to look into the water. What do you see? You notice that water is entering this pool from the top of the bank, and you intuitively know this flow represents the money flow in your life. How does it flow?

As you watch the water, you see three blocks interrupting its flow. Each block represents an issue impeding the flow of money into your life. You walk up the slope and stand next to the first block. You sense what this represents in your life. When you are ready, you move it. The water flows faster and with more purpose before it is interrupted by the second block. Again, you sense the connection with your own life circumstances and move it.

You are unable to move the last block. You sense its roots are hidden deep in the earth and that you are tied to this block. As you look to the top of the bank, you see a figure watching you. This is your guardian, the lord of your second house. They move towards you, explaining that this last block has invisible cords connected to you and if you want to be released, you have to choose to release these cords.

They ask you to imagine what life would look and feel like without financial blocks. As they talk, these invisible cords start to become visible and you see where they are being held within your body. Your guide asks if you are ready to cut these cords. When you agree, you notice the block immediately releasing, rolling away, clearing the path for the water to flow into the pool.

With the blocks removed, the water runs smoothly with increased tempo and the pool becomes larger, deeper and more alive. Your guardian says that this water will be able to resource different areas of your life. As you look into the pool, you see underground tunnels directing the flow of water, a natural flow of water entering and leaving the pool.

Your guardian says that it's time to leave, but you can return to this place whenever you wish to reroute the flow of water or simply to feel resourced from this energy of abundance. You follow the path back through nature, hearing the calls of the wild and the flow of your water behind you. When you arrive at the door, you knock three times, returning to the large circle. The second house door closes behind you.

The Third House

Ages

2 | 14 | 26 | 38 | 50 | 62 | 74 | 86

Keywords

Mind, learning, siblings

Element

Air

Mantra

I communicate with clarity
and confidence, nurture my curiosity
and build meaningful connections
in my everyday life.

The Third House environment

☽ ● ☾

THE THIRD HOUSE has been traditionally connected to the concrete mind, dealing with everyday thoughts and your familiar, rational mental activities. It focuses on how you perceive and communicate with the world around you. This house is often linked to childhood experiences, particularly those from your early school years.

Learning usually starts in school, making those years a central aspect of the third house. How you take in information, your default learning style and the types of things that interest you are all important themes here. As you grow older, the third house also covers the brief communications in your daily routine, such as the magazines you read, the social media accounts you follow and the books you enjoy.

❝❞
The GREATEST thing in life is to keep your mind young.
Henry Ford

Siblings are also part of the third house since their presence (or absence) significantly influences your upbringing. While parents have their own designated houses (the fourth and tenth), the third house includes all blood relatives and neighbours. This encompasses everyone who plays a part in your everyday, from the postman and fellow dog walker to the person you see regularly at the bus stop.

The third house is best summed up as your 'everyday environment'. It represents how you interact with life outside of your front door. Your unique mindset means you have a different day-to-day experience compared to others, as you perceive and communicate with your environment and the people within it in your own way.

Entering your Third House year

Overview

THIS IS THE YEAR when your mind is under the spotlight so it's a great time to look at your habitual thoughts and how these influence your day-to-day life. Any outdated thought patterns will be easier to transform so notice how your mindset could be holding you back and pro-actively seek ways to change this when you enter a third house year.

Communication is a central theme so spend time looking at how you communicate and how well understood you feel. Any effort that you invest in your mind will pay dividends, whether that takes the form of learning, teaching or varying the information sources that currently shape your opinions.

Re-exploring your neighbourhood and the people that you share it with is also part of the third house experience. This is a great opportunity to rethink the normal routines that occur in the world outside your front door as small changes will have far reaching benefits.

Finally, siblings are included in the third house so looking back at how these family members have previously featured in past third house visits will be helpful.

House support

Journaling: Journaling is a powerful tool for your third house year. Establishing a daily writing ritual enhances self-awareness by helping you understand and analyze your unconscious thought patterns. This practice will also provide you with deeper insights into your interactions with your everyday environment.

Learn a new skill: This is a brilliant year to expand your mind and learn a new skill. You may find that you are naturally more curious about a specific topic and wish to self-educate or re-enter formal education in some way. It may be useful to think back to school and consider reactivating any dormant subjects that you once particularly liked and engaged with.

Tapping: Tapping, also known as EFT (Emotional Freedom Technique) is one way to effortlessly change your thought patterns in the moment. Based on Chinese acupressure and modern psychology, tapping involves using your fingertips to 'tap' on specific meridian points in your face and neck. There are many videos online that show you different ways to use this method.

Third House

Journal prompts

How did my experiences in school shape my current approach to learning and communication?

What lessons did I learn from my siblings? How have they impacted my personal development?

How does my current environment influence my thoughts? What changes can I make to improve this?

What recurring thoughts or beliefs do I have? How do they impact my daily life?

How do I express my thoughts and feelings? What can I do to improve my communication skills?

A Third House Activity
Neighbourhood connections

It's easy to zone out during familiar routines in your day-to-day life. When I worked in public relations, I spent three years driving the same 40-minute route from my home to the office. This drive became so habitual that I often had little recollection of the journey once I arrived.

Realizing the dangers of this mindset, I began changing my morning commute. I took different routes, left earlier to walk part of the way and began to use public transport. Not only did I remember my journey more, but I also became increasingly aware of the world and people around me.

While the automated state is common, it leaves no room for spontaneity or joy. This exercise is designed to reawaken you to the world outside of your front door and show how your habitual or awakened mindset influences your perception of it.

Time: 30 minutes–1 hour
Tools: Pack of 10–20 plain postcards.

1. Draw your states:
* On one side of a postcard, draw an image that represents you in a habitual mode and write any words you associate with this state.
* On the other side, draw an image that represents you in an awakened state and write any keywords associated with this experience.

2. Explore your neighbourhood:
* Take a walk around your neighbourhood, visiting familiar places as well as areas you haven't explored.
* At each location, pause and observe your surroundings. Note the details, sounds and feelings you experience.
* On a postcard, draw one side representing your environment from a habitual state and the other from an awakened state. Note any observations and feelings associated with each state.

3. Engage with your community:

✱ During your exploration, engage with at least one person you encounter. This could be a neighbour, a shop owner or a passerby. Have a brief conversation and note how it makes you feel.

✱ On a postcard, reflect on this interaction and how your mindset influenced the communication.

4. Journaling:

✱ After your exploration, journal about your experience. Reflect on how your habitual and awakened states differed in perceiving the same environment.

✱ Write about any new insights or changes in perspective you gained.

5. Plan for change:

✱ Based on your reflections, identify one or two changes you can make to break out of habitual routines and stay more awakened in your daily life.

66 99

You must PLAN to be SPONTANEOUS.

David Hockney

A Third House **Meditation**
Transforming thought patterns & perceptions

Begin with the relaxation exercise on page 12.

Crystal: Blue lace agate
Essential oil: Peppermint

You find yourself standing in the middle of a large circle surrounded by 12 doors. Each of these doors has a number on it. You notice that the door with the number three on it is pulsating and you are strongly drawn to move towards it. There is a key already in the lock. Turn the key and step over the doorway into your third house. You find yourself in a bright, airy classroom. A sign at the front reads 'This room is specifically created for excelled learning'.

The room is filled with natural light and you see several windows. Outside, clouds drift by, giving you a sense of being high up, offering a broad vantage point of the world below.

You notice multiple desks and chairs and choose one to sit at. At the front of the room is a tall figure and you instinctively know that this is the guardian of your third house. They welcome you warmly, saying they have been expecting you.

Your guardian walks over and together you watch a large screen. An image of yourself as a child in your school uniform appears. The scenes shift to memories of your school years: classrooms, the playground and the moments of school pick-ups and drop-offs.

Your guardian explains that during those years, you adopted certain beliefs about learning that no longer serve you. They go on to explain that these beliefs have limited your mental abilities. As they speak, they place their hand just above your crown, hovering over the centre of your head. You feel a tingling sensation and an increased sense of lightness.

Your guardian tells you that the blocks to receiving information have been lifted. Then they place their hand in front of your eyes and again you feel a rush of energy and lightness. Opening your eyes, you experience a fresh, clear view of the world around you.

Your guardian tells you that it's time to re-open the door to your mind, to delve into an area of life you feel drawn to understand in more detail. They assure you that this exploration will enhance your life, helping you see yourself and others in a new way.

The screen flickers to life again, showing you as you are now, but in a vibrant learning environment. You see yourself reading, writing and talking to people who share your interests.

Your guardian places in your hand the key that was originally in the door. They say that this third house classroom will remain unlocked for you throughout this year. You can return at any time for support and guidance; they will always be ready and expecting you. You thank your guardian for their healing and leave your desk, exiting through the door you entered. As you step over the doorway you hear the third house door gently close behind you.

The Fourth House

Ages

3 | 15 | 27 | 39 | 51 | 63 | 75 | 87

Keywords
Home, roots, belonging

Element
Water

Mantra
My home is my sanctuary.
Within these walls, I am supported,
guided and inspired by the enduring
light of my ancestors.

The Fourth House environment

☽ ● ☾

AS THE MOST PRIVATE HOUSE, traditionally this was the house that was referred to as being at the 'bottom of the heavens'. Found at the base of the wheel, this is the least visible of all the astrological houses and holds the essence of retreat, where you seek sanctuary and replenishment.

Home and roots are key themes of the fourth house – both your inner home, reflecting how safe and secure you feel within yourself, and your physical home. This house represents the place where the hidden parts of yourself are kept, including behaviours that occur behind closed doors rather than in public.

Past homes also belong here; your childhood home and the associated atmospheres that were absorbed when growing up as well as the homes that belonged to your ancestors. The origins of your family are held in the fourth house and this would include any countries that were once considered home.

Along with the tenth house, the fourth house is part of the parental axis. There is some debate about which parent this house signifies. As the most hidden house, some astrologers believe it represents the father, traditionally the more hidden parent, while others see it as the natural place for the mother. As family structures evolve, it is more helpful to view this house as representing the least visible caregiver rather than a specific parent.

In addition to representing your ancestral genetics, the fourth house also signifies your legacy – what will you leave behind and be remembered for? Recognized for its association with endings, both materially and physically, this house reveals how you experience letting go and completion.

❝❞

CONNECTION is
why we're here.
Brené Brown

Entering your Fourth House year

Overview

WHEN ENTERING A fourth house year, themes connected to home are likely to surface in some form. This might involve your physical home, where you seek refuge, or it could be more psychological, bringing up issues related to your ancestral or childhood homes.

Reflecting on your roots is particularly valuable this year, as it's an ideal time to deepen connections with places that bring you peace and calm. Feelings around belonging may also emerge, prompting you to explore where and with whom you feel most at home.

Since the fourth house is linked to parents, themes involving your mother and father, their parenting and your early home life may come up. It's useful to consider how life was during your last fourth house year and observe how you've evolved over the past 12 years.

Aligned with endings, a fourth house year often brings natural conclusions. You may find that people, relationships or situations from your youth reach a resolution. While this might evoke feelings of loss, allowing these completions is crucial during a fourth house year to ensure energetic ties are fully resolved.

House support

Feng Shi: In Feng Shui, focusing on the family area of your home can help you honour your ancestors and elevate the energy in your living space. Concentrate on the eastern part of your home, which is traditionally linked to family and health. You can enhance this space with plants, family photos and items in soothing colours to symbolize growth and vitality.

Ancestral journaling: As your ancestors are found in the fourth house, any exploration of their lives can help expand your experience of this year. You can write about your earliest memories of home and family life and interview older family members to learn more about your ancestry. Reflect on how your family history has shaped your sense of self and belonging and explore any recurring family themes that influence your current life.

House harmony: Each physical home has its own energetic field and this is influenced by the land it was built on as well as past occupants. Negative emotions may be cleared by a 'house healer' – they will clear the emotional shadows by cleansing the house's field.

Fourth House
Journal prompts

How do I define the concept of 'home'? What makes a place feel like home to me?

Reflect on a significant ending in my life. How did it affect me? What did I learn from it?

How do I honour my ancestors and their legacy in my life?

What aspects of my personal history do I want to explore and understand better?

What past experiences am I holding onto? How can I begin to let go of them?

A Fourth House Activity
Creating an ancestral altar

When I lived in Thailand, I was struck by the beautiful altars found outside homes, shops and restaurants as well as those at the sides of the roads. These altars honoured the spirits that occupied the space and I loved how the past was respected in this way.

Honouring those that came before you can be a powerful ritual connected to your own lineage. My current altar in my house is dedicated to my maternal grandfather. I knew him when I was growing up and since he died over 20 years ago, I've often thought about his life, especially his own experiences of being in the Second World War.

My altar is simple, it has several photos of him at different stages in his life. I have a bookmark under one of the photos as he was a great reader and always encouraged us to read by taking my sister and I to the local bookshop. I have also placed a grey feather in front and a candle.

Occasionally, I change the items, adding different family members to acknowledge and express gratitude to them, recognizing that their lives paved the way for my own. Creating your own altar is personal to you. Instead of following a rigid format, I believe your ancestors engage more easily through your intuition and signs that have personal meaning.

Time: 20 minutes–1 hour
Tools: Smudge stick (optional) Photograph/s, personal items that have meaning.

**Steps to create
your ancestral altar**

1. Choose a space:
✴ Select an area in your home that you feel drawn to.

2. Clear the area:
✴ Remove any clutter.
✴ If you have sage, smudge the area or simply open a window to clear the air.
3. Select ancestors:
✴ Think about the ancestors

you feel particularly connected to at this time.

* You may focus on one ancestor or include many, even if you never met them but sense their positive support in your life.

4. Gather items:

* Collect items that you associate with them, such as photographs and personal belongings. If you don't have photos, use objects or materials that remind you of their presence and life.

5. Create the altar:

* Arrange these items in a way that feels right to you, creating a space that honours and remembers them.
* There's no set timescale for how long to keep your altar. Trust what feels right for you, knowing that strengthening your bond with your ancestors also strengthens the flow of support through your family lineage.

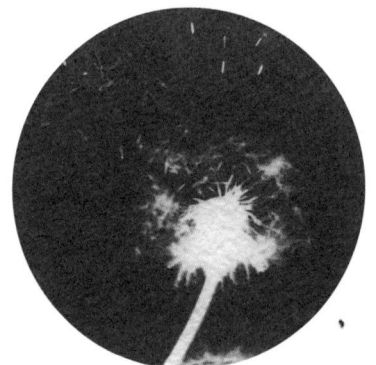

66 99

Receiving from the PAST, we can give to the FUTURE.

Joanna Macy

A Fourth House Meditation

A guided tour of your home's hidden depths

Begin with the relaxation exercise on page 12.

Crystal: Black tourmaline
Essential oil: Cedarwood

You find yourself standing within a vast circle, encircled by 12 numbered doors. From the middle of the circle you can see that door number four lies directly ahead. You walk up to the door, but as you search for the door handle you become aware that you can't see it. Sensing the presence of another, you look to your side and see your guardian, the lord of your fourth house beside you. What do they look like? How comfortable and familiar do you feel in their presence? The guide tells you that the door handle is hidden but the door will open if you take a moment to visualize your fourth house door keepers.

Close your eyes and allow your mind to bring forth images of people who are the door keepers to this part of your life. In your mind you see a group of men and women standing behind you. You realize these people are directly connected to your family line and if it were not for them you would not be the person that you are. Gratefully acknowledging their unseen influence, the door swings open and you move through it, into the fourth house portal.

You emerge into darkness, sensing that you are underground in some form of basement. A candle slowly flickers to life, revealing the spirit – a guide of your current home. This guide explains their bond with your home and invites you on a tour to unveil its hidden facets.

Ascending the stairs, daylight greets you once more. The house bustles with daily activities, oblivious to your presence beside your guide. The guide tells you that the house has an energy of its own and reveals three potent spots: two downstairs and one upstairs. Each spot pulsates with a distinct energy, resonating deeply within your awareness.

As you move around your house, specific objects appear to have an aura and radiate a light, high energy. You notice that there are some objects that emit a beautiful feeling and others that emit a darker, less positive frequency. Your guardian points to objects that aren't an energetic fit with your home and would be better placed outside of your house.

After the tour, you follow your guide back to the basement. The guide explains what the house needs to thrive in order to increase its support and care of each occupant.

With gratitude, you bid farewell to the guide, preparing to depart from your fourth house. Stepping back through the portal, you gently close the door behind you and return to the familiar space of the circle.

66 99

To FORGET one's ANCESTORS is to be a brook without a SOURCE, a tree without a root.

Chinese proverb

The
Fifth House

Ages

4 | 16 | 28 | 40 | 52 | 64 | 76 | 88

Keywords

**Pleasure, creativity,
self-expression**

Element

Fire

Mantra

**I embrace joy, creativity and the light
of my inner child, allowing pleasure
and love to guide my journey.**

The Fifth House environment

☽ ● ☾

WHILE THE FIFTH HOUSE may initially seem to be made up of a variety of somewhat unrelated themes, it is actually underpinned by the notion of pleasure. This house represents the part of life where activities are chosen for the fun and entertainment that they bring into your life. This is all about the things that you love doing, just for the pure joy of it rather than for survival or external success. Anything that makes you feel alive, energized and the centre of your own universe belongs in the fifth house.

Romance is strongly connected to this house. It is where you'd place the early stages of love, the blissful honeymoon period when you surrender to the moment rather than focusing on results or future commitments. While the seventh house deals with committed relationships, the fifth house is interested in your pleasure and how special and radiant this connection makes you feel.

> **" "**
> Your HEART knows the WAY. Run in that DIRECTION.
> **Rumi**

Creativity is also strongly linked to this house. I always think of this dwelling as the home of 'what only you can give birth to'. This naturally includes children and also all forms of creativity, especially how you express your heart energy and the form it takes when released into the world.

Finally, gambling, investment and speculation are also included in this placement, which may seem somewhat unrelated at first. However, remembering that this house is about expressing pleasure helps clarify this connection. For many, taking risks, especially around money, brings a sense of excitement and (initial) pleasure.

Entering your Fifth House year

Overview

THIS IS A POWERFUL YEAR to focus on your pleasure and creativity. You are likely to find that you want to have fun and are more proactive in creating this in your life. As a fire house (like the first and ninth), the fifth year allows you to tap into a dynamic flow that enables you to prioritize your personal desires. Think about the things that you love doing, especially those things you loved when you were a child and create time to engage in these activities more frequently.

As the house of love affairs, you may well find that you gain more attention in this area and while not necessarily long term, this is a great year of sensual exploration and satisfaction.

Children are also likely to feature prominently this year. If you don't have children, they may start appearing on your radar, and if you do, their presence will be felt more strongly.

Ultimately, this is your year to prioritize your heart. Situations, people and relationships that obstruct your heart flow will become impossible to ignore and are likely to fade away.

House support

Writing a letter to your younger self: Childhood belongs to the fifth house so spending time nurturing your inner child is hugely beneficial. This can be from re-reading a favourite book to looking at your old childhood photos. Taking a moment to write to your younger self is also powerful – giving advice and supporting them with words that you once needed to hear.

A love affair: As the fifth house is about love affairs, this is your year to fall in love with yourself. View yourself as the object of your greatest desires and consider the ways that you could enhance the pleasure in your life. If you just met *you*, what would you like to do? This is your year to make time for you, whether it is candlelit baths or carefully prepared food, find creative ways to love yourself.

Play: If there was ever a time to play, this would be it; have fun for the sake of it. Consider the things you enjoyed when you were young – fly a kite, jump in puddles, dance in the rain, buy colouring pencils or playdough – just notice what play looks like to you and create space and time to express your heart energy out into the world.

Fifth House
Journal prompts

How much space is there in my life for spontaneity?

How can I reconnect with the sense of wonder and imagination I had as a child?

When did I last laugh?

How comfortable am I allowing play just for the sake of it?

How open is my heart to receiving love? What past experiences might be influencing my ability to accept love fully?

A Fifth House Activity
Creating your life's journey with peg dolls

This activity involves creating different representations of yourself at the ages you were or will be when you enter the fifth house.

Time: 1–3 hours
Tools: 7 plain wooden peg dolls, markers, paint, felt, fabric, 7 plain postcards

1. Four years old:
* Start with the first wooden peg doll, which represents you at four years old. Using markers, paint, felt or fabric, decorate this doll to represent your four-year-old self. Once it is completed, ask your four-year-old self what it needs to thrive and have fun. Notice the words or thoughts that come forth. Write down these words or themes on a plain postcard and place the peg doll on top of it.

2. Sixteen years old:
* Repeat the process for the next peg doll, representing you at sixteen. Decorate the doll, then reflect on what your sixteen-year-old self needs to thrive. Write down these insights on a postcard and place the peg doll on it.

3. Twenty-eight years old:
* Decorate the third peg doll to represent you at twenty-eight. Consider what your twenty-eight-year-old self needs for fulfilment and joy. Note these thoughts on a postcard and place the peg doll on it.

4. Forty years old:
* For the fourth peg doll, imagine yourself at forty. Decorate the doll and reflect on what is important for you at this stage of life. Write down these reflections on a postcard and place the peg doll on it.

5. Fifty-two years old:
* The fifth peg doll represents you at fifty-two. Decorate it and consider the needs and desires of your fifty-two-year-old self. Write these on a postcard and place the peg doll on it.

6. Sixty-four years old:

✴ Decorate the sixth peg doll to represent you at sixty-four. Reflect on what is significant for you at this age. Record these insights on a postcard and place the peg doll on it.

7. Seventy-six years old:

✴ This peg doll represents you at seventy-six. Use your imagination and intuition to visualize your life at this age. Note what is important to you on a postcard and place the peg doll on it.

8. Eighty-eight years old:

✴ Now imagine yourself at eighty-eight years old. Consider how you would like your life to be. What would bring you joy? How can this be reflected in your peg doll?

Whether you've reached these ages or not, use your intuition to guide your creations. Reflect on what might be important to you at each stage of life and enjoy this journey through your personal timeline.

66 99

Find out where
JOY resides, and
give it a VOICE...

Robert Louis Stevenson

A Fifth House Meditation
Journey to the meadow of joy

Begin with the relaxation exercise on page 12.

Crystal: Rose quartz
Essential oil: Wild orange

You find yourself standing in a large circle, surrounded by 12 doors with numbers on them. You walk towards the fifth house door and stand outside it. The door is bright red with a large number five. You turn the handle and step inside.

You find yourself standing inside a large tree. The trunk of the tree opens like a door and you step outside into a large meadow. The meadow stretches out before you, a vast expanse of lush green grass dotted with vibrant wildflowers and bordered by tall ancient trees. A bubbling brook meanders through the field and you notice the soothing sound of bird song. Bathed in warm, golden sunlight under a brilliant blue sky, the meadow feels like a serene haven of peace and natural beauty.

You see a line of baby rabbits hopping towards you, with their mother rabbit following close behind. You sit on the grass, and the rabbits come closer. You start playing with them, enjoying the softness of their fur.

Two figures appear in the meadow. One is a small child, the other a taller figure. The taller figure walks over and introduces themself as the guardian of your fifth house. They explain that the child is you. You watch your younger self completely absorbed in the wonders of nature. After a while, your younger self notices you and skips over to where you are sitting.

You feel an immediate sense of love, protection and care as you welcome your younger self. With your guardian by your side, you sit in a circle with the rabbits, and more animals and their babies gradually join you. You ask your younger self what they enjoy the most and they tell you about their favourite activities.

You notice a rose quartz crystal next to you, glowing with a gentle pink hue. When you pick it up, you feel a warm, soothing sensation in your hand. Rose quartz is known for its pure form of love and you pass the crystal to your younger self, telling them it is a symbol of your unconditional love. Your younger self holds the crystal joyfully, then notices a feather floating by. Soon, more feathers are drifting in the wind, and your younger self chases after them.

You ask if they want to invite any friends to the meadow and they eagerly list several names. These friends soon appear, and you watch your younger self laugh, run and play with them. Your guardian turns to you with a warm smile and says, 'It's time for you to laugh more in your life, to chase feathers and to embrace the joy and lightness of being. You don't have to be serious all the time. Allow yourself to play, to explore and to reconnect with the carefree spirit of your younger self. This year you are more connected to your younger self than ever before and it's important to let that connection guide you towards more happiness and spontaneity.'

Before you leave, you take one last look at the vast meadow, knowing you'll revisit it in your dreams.

You walk back to the tree and open the trunk door. As it closes, you find yourself back outside the fifth house door and gently close it behind you.

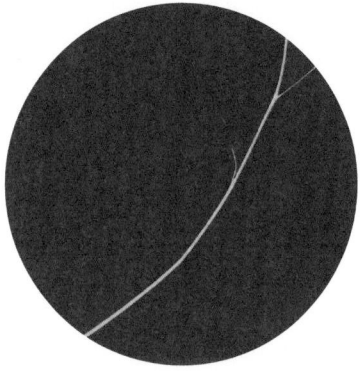

❝ ❞

We need JOY as we need air. We need LOVE as we need water. We need EACH OTHER as we need the Earth we share.

Maya Angelou

The Sixth House

Ages

5 | 17 | 29 | 41 | 53 | 65 | 77 | 89

Keywords

Health, day-to-day
work, service

Element

Earth

Mantra

Through practice and preparation,
I find harmony and health.

The Sixth House environment

☽ ● ☾

THE ANCIENT ASTROLOGERS called the sixth house the 'house of slavery'. This was seen as one of the 'bad houses' and themes of subjection, sickness and physical infirmity were placed firmly at the sixth house door. However, modern astrology, which doesn't believe in bad houses, sees this placement differently. While servitude and service are part of this house experience, it is more connected to the daily duties and routines that may feel arduous but actually enable you to survive in the moment and potentially thrive in the future.

Day-to-day work is one of the strongest themes linked to this house. Seen as the workhouse, this placement reveals your attitude and approach to everyday work, especially what you need to do to put food on the table. Relationships within the workplace are also found here, whether as an employer or employee. This is also the area of your life where you are navigating unequal relationships; where you can benefit from the labours of others, or others are benefiting directly from your hard work.

> **❝❞**
> Drop by drop
> is the water
> pot FILLED.
> **Buddha**

Health is an important part of the sixth house. This links to work as traditionally if you were well, you could work and if you weren't, then you couldn't. Unlike the first house, which is concerned with your appearance and vitality, the sixth house is looking at what blocks your health and your ability to survive. Issues that arise here are often connected to how well you 'service' and look after your body in your everyday life and illnesses that arise are often connected to overwork.

Finally, small animals and pets belong in the sixth house. Some astrologers believe this was related to when animals were used in service for activities such as hunting, guarding properties or catching vermin. However, current thinking is that pets are part of day-to-day life and looking after their needs is part of our daily routine.

Entering your Sixth House year

Overview

THIS IS AN IMPORTANT YEAR to think about how you have set up your day-to-day life. It's very easy to get caught in habitual behaviours which were once adopted for necessity but are kept in place for familiarity. Taking time to step back and look at your bigger vision is useful as you can assess how your routines support or distract the directions that you wish your life to go in.

As your daily work is connected to this house it is also useful to evaluate the tasks that you do and see if there are more efficient ways to gain the same or better results. How you relate to your employment is likely to be on your radar and you may notice that there are changes in your working relationships.

Health is also under the celestial spotlight this year. This doesn't mean that you'll become ill or have a health scare, but it does mean that you'll start to reconsider how you look after your physical wellbeing in some way. Ultimately this is a great time to prioritize your body and introduce new daily habits that will support your wellness.

House support

Health MOT: As health is centre stage this year, it's worth being proactive and seeking out knowledge for your current state of wellbeing. There are many types of health assessments available and it is useful to explore what resonates for you. As this house is seen to have similarities with the sign of Virgo, focusing on your gut health is beneficial as this is the area of your body that this sign rules.

Life coach: Investing in your own self-development is especially useful this year. This is an ideal time to work with an expert to analyze the routines and beliefs that underpin your day-to-day life. With fresh insight it is often easier to make changes that will bring more meaning and purpose to your life.

Spending time with animals: As small animals belong to the sixth house you may find that they feature more prominently in your life. For some, it may be getting a new pet, while for others it may be that you find yourself looking after someone else's. Or, as this is also a year related to service, you may find yourself drawn to volunteering at a local animal rescue centre.

Sixth House

Journal prompts

How do my daily habits impact my physical and mental health?

How important is self-care in my day-to-day routine?

How does my current work align with my long-term career goals?

How do I respond to criticism or feedback from colleagues?

How fulfilling is my everyday life?

A Sixth House Activity
Your footprints of life

Time: 30 minutes
Tools: Large pieces of paper, scissors, pencils and colouring pens.

1. Footprint one: Reflecting on past steps

* The first footprint represents all the footprints you have made in your life. Think about how your day-to-day small steps have led to bigger, life-changing steps. Reflect on times when you were scared but still stepped forward, when you took leaps of faith and the smaller daily steps you take to support and care for those you love. Write down examples on this footprint.

* Turn the footprint over and think about your hidden footprints, the ones that don't always get acknowledged but significantly impact how life moves forward. On the sole of the footprint, note some of these unseen footprints. This could include supermarket trips, tax returns or daily dog walks. While they may not be the most exciting activities, they play a critical part in your day-to-day life.

2. Footprint two: Envisioning future steps

* The second footprint represents the steps you have yet to take. Think about the next time you enter a sixth house year and all the steps you will have made during these 12 years.

* In alignment with what is most important to you, write on the sole of the second footprint what these next steps are. Include steps that will move you forward in your work, health and well-being. Consider what new steps you would include, what steps you would remove and what you would like your day-to-day life to look like.

A Sixth House **Meditation**
Invoking health and harmony

Follow the basic relaxation meditation on page 12.

Crystal: Amethyst
Essential oil: Lavender

You find yourself inside a large circle surrounded by 12 different doors each with different numbers on them. You are immediately drawn to the sixth house door and walk towards it. Your guide, the guardian of your sixth house appears beside you and unlocks the door. What does your guide look like? How do you feel standing next to them?

Your guide waits for you to open the door and you both enter the sixth house. You find yourself in a long corridor with windows all along the left-hand side. You look through the windows – what do you see?

In front of you are people standing in a queue. As they wait to move through a door a photograph is taken of them. Your guide asks you to follow them and moves you to the front of the queue. As you wait in line, your photograph is taken and after this, the door opens. As you enter the room with your

guide, you see a figure sitting in a chair. You are struck by how much light surrounds this person and notice how delighted they are to see you. Your guide tells you that they are a healer, a revered doctor of energetic medicine. In their hand, the healer holds a large photograph of your body, they tell you that certain areas of your body are experiencing stress from your day-to-day choices. The healer shows you where this ill-ease is positioned on your body and gives you advice on what your body needs. What do they say?

As you leave the room, your guide takes you through a different door, and you find yourself in a lift. Your guide presses number six and you find yourself moving upwards. As you arrive on the sixth floor you immediately hear soothing music. Your guide tells you that the frequency of this music is for divine healing. They walk you to a chair, and you sit down. Six beings of light surround you, and you feel a great wave of lightness enter your body, starting at the crown and moving like a gentle breeze down to your feet. You bask in this warmth, feeling elevated, pure and safe.

After a time, you find yourself more conscious of your body, as if you are landing back home again. The six beings of light have left you and your body is tingly; you are aware of a deep sense of ease and peace flowing through you. You leave the chair and with your guide go back down in the lift.

You find yourself heading back towards the door that you first entered. You and your guide step through the sixth house portal and hear it close behind you. You step back into the circle and are ready to re-enter your day-to-day life.

66 99

You find PEACE not by rearranging the circumstances of your life, but by REALIZING who you are...

Eckhart Tolle

The Seventh House

Ages

6 | 18 | 30 | 42 | 54 | 66 | 78 | 90

Keywords

Relationships, the other,
open enemies

Element

Air

Mantra

I embrace balance and harmony in
all my relationships, nurturing mutual
understanding and growth.

The Seventh House environment

☽ ● ☾

THE SEVENTH HOUSE represents your significant relationships, such as long-term romantic partners or business partners. Unlike the eleventh house, which focuses on your broader social circle or 'clan', the seventh house is about those who have a committed and meaningful presence in your life.

The seventh house is directly opposite the first house, which is all about your own identity and self. While the first house focuses on who you are as an individual, the seventh house is connected to the qualities you don't see in yourself. When you are attracted to someone, it can feel like they possess a missing ingredient, a quality that you don't have, which creates a sense of wholeness.

However, part of the seventh house experience is understanding that this is a projection. The so-called missing trait you see in others is actually an unconscious part of yourself that you find difficult to accept. Once you acknowledge and develop these seventh house qualities within yourself, you will feel more complete and your relationships will become more balanced and harmonious.

The seventh house is also linked to open enemies. During these times, the seventh house can feel like a battlefield. Understanding that the tension can be due to not owning all parts of yourself, and seeking commonality with your opponent can help you navigate these challenging relationships more effectively.

The seventh house is about the development and growth you achieve through others. This includes learning from others, especially from those that feel like 'the other'. However, it's important to remember that you always view significant others through your own seventh house lens, rather than seeing them objectively for who they truly are.

66 99

He who lives in harmony with HIMSELF lives in harmony with the UNIVERSE.

Marcus Aurelius

Entering your Seventh House year

Overview

WHEN YOU ARE ENTERING a seventh house year, relationships are at the top of your menu. While this can mean meeting new people who become significant in work or love, it can also mean that your current relationships change leading to either transformation or completion.

This year you are resourced to focus on how you relate to others so any effort that you proactively put into this area of your life is beneficial. Many people use this as an opportunity to explore and clear unconscious blocks that are hindering the type of relationships that they are looking to create. This could include being energetically tied to a previous partner or fearing what it would mean to be truly available to someone else and thus unconsciously sabotaging what it is that you truly wish for.

While this is not the case for everyone, you could find that the seventh house year brings conflict to your door. While this isn't necessarily comfortable, it is a great opportunity to look deeper at the causes of this tension so that you can learn about any hidden parts of yourself that are showing up through this particular 'partnership'.

House support

Love languages: The book *The 5 Love Languages* by Gary Chapman describes five different love languages – words of affirmation, quality time, gifts, acts of service and physical touch. Most people will tend to have one main language with a second one as a backup. Understanding your love language and your own relationship needs is incredibly useful in enhancing harmony and understanding within your connections.

Past life healing: Sometimes problems that emerge within relationships are not linked to this lifetime. If you are experiencing repeated unwanted patterns then it may be that the solution does not belong in the rational world. If you are open to the belief that this is one life of many, then past life therapy can be beneficial in clearing past attachments or beliefs.

Love list: If you are wishing to create a new love or work relationship, then writing a list of the qualities that you desire this person to have is incredibly powerful. This works particularly well under a New Moon as it is the most potent time to sow new seeds.

Seventh House

Journal prompts

What recurring patterns do I notice in my significant relationships? What do they reveal about my own inner dynamics?

How do I balance my needs and identity with those of my partner in a relationship?

What qualities do I admire in my closest relationships? How can I develop these qualities within myself?

Can I improve my relationships by seeing my partners for who they truly are, rather than through the lens of my own expectations and projections?

In what ways do I express love and affection? Does this expression align with my partner's needs?

A Seventh House Activity

Understanding the energy flow in your relationships

This activity allows you to explore and visualize the dynamics of your significant relationships. By mapping out these connections, you can gain insights into what each person brings to your life and reflect on the qualities you project in return. This exercise encourages a deeper understanding and growth in your connections.

Time: 30 minutes
Tools: Paper, pens.

1. Prepare your paper
* Take a large piece of paper and draw an image of yourself in the centre.

2. Draw close connections
* Identify four to six people who are closest to you in your life.
* Draw each of these people on the paper around your central image.
* Draw arrows from these people to yourself.
* Write down words or sentences along these arrows that describe what these individuals bring to your life and how their presence benefits you.

3. Identify challenging connections
* Think of four to six people who are not close to you and whom you would prefer not to spend time with.
* Add these individuals to your drawing.
* Draw arrows from these people to yourself.
* Reflect on any benefits or insights you have gained from their presence, such as lessons learned or new understandings about yourself or life. Write these reflections along the arrows.

4. Reflect on your qualities
* Consider the qualities you radiate to both groups of people.
* Think about how your energy flows and what you could do to enhance these connections.

" "
INDIVIDUALLY, we are
one drop. TOGETHER,
we are an OCEAN.
Ryunosuke Satoro

A Seventh House Meditation
Cutting the hidden bonds in relationships

Follow the basic relaxation meditation on page 12.

Crystal: Rhodonite
Essential oil: Rose

You find yourself standing in the centre of a large circle. Around you are 12 doors. You notice that the seventh door is humming and you are immediately drawn towards it. You take in the unique colour and texture of the door. As you stand by the door, you are joined by a figure that tells you that they are your seventh house guardian. They are here to take you on a journey of great healing.

You push the door open and both of you walk through the seventh house portal. You find yourself in a beautiful forest – the tall trees stand dignified and all around you can hear the sounds of the forest – the birds, the trees, all the inhabitants of this vast world. You look up to the blue sky and see an eagle soaring free above you.

As you survey the forest, you see two large wooden thrones. The thrones have been carved out of a tree. You sit in one throne and your guardian sits next to you as a reassuring and protective presence. You notice rustling and see a figure walking towards you. You immediately recognize this figure as a person from your past, they were one of your most cherished friends from childhood. Your childhood friend stands in front of you and thanks you for such positive memories and shares visions of the happiness that they gained from you. You find yourself also thanking them and tell them what you gained and learned about life because of that friendship.

As the childhood friend leaves, you notice another person from your past coming towards you. This person isn't connected to such positive experiences and you notice your body tense. Your guide places a hand on your shoulder and tells you that even though this person felt like an opponent, you were both similar as your behaviours came from a similar fear and wound. Even though this person isn't in your life there is still a cord that keeps you unconsciously tied to them and the emotions that they initially stirred at the time. Your guide asks you to see them differently, to imagine that you are looking in a mirror that shows aspects of yourself that are normally hidden.

As you look into this person's eyes, you see a familiarity based on pain. You share with this person how it was knowing them and how with the gift of hindsight the experience has influenced your life. This person also shares their experience and learnings. You see a cord from your body connected to their body. Your guide cuts it and frees you both from the past.

As they leave, you feel calmer and notice that another person is walking towards you. This is the person that you had your first relationship with. You both talk about what you gained from it and how it influenced the person that you are. Again, you notice a cord connecting you both and your guide says that it is time to cut it.

As they leave, you see one more person heading towards you. This is the person that you have struggled to let go of emotionally. Even though you aren't in a relationship with them, you find yourself energetically pulled back to them. You speak honestly with the person and your guide cuts the cord. You are both free to experience love in the way that is appropriate and true for the person that you are now.

As you get ready to leave the forest, you notice there is a deep sense of lightness and freedom. The eagle flies high above you, leading you back to the portal door of the seventh house. You and your guardian step through it and you hear the door close behind you.

The Eighth House

Ages

7 | 19 | 31 | 43 | 55 | 67 | 79 | 91

Keywords

Intimacy, secrets, death,
other people's money

Element

Water

Mantra

I trust in the cycles of death
and rebirth within me, knowing
that each ending brings valuable
lessons and each new beginning
holds limitless potential.

The Eighth House environment

THE EIGHTH HOUSE is the deepest, darkest and most private of all astrological houses. Themes associated with this house are often intense, taboo or secretive. As a water house, it connects to the parts of your life where you must trust your intuition, as the events that occur here have the power to transform and change you forever.

Positioned opposite the second house of money, the eighth house focuses on the resources of others, especially within the dynamics of relationships when reserves, often financial, are merged. This merging can invoke unconscious power issues, making the eighth house's energy about what happens after you have invested yourself physically, emotionally and financially with someone else. Intimacy and shared resources are key aspects of this house, making it a powerful influence on forming new relationships or deepening existing ones.

Inheritance is also a significant aspect of this placement. While financial inheritance is commonly highlighted, karmic inheritance is equally important, encompassing issues that have been suppressed, rejected or ignored within the family line.

As the house of mystery and the occult, death has always been strongly associated with the eighth house. Historically, astrologers would use this house to foretell death, but as 'death readings' are now considered taboo and ethically wrong, the eighth house is currently viewed as representing symbolic death.

This symbolic death refers to the shedding of your identity, where painful circumstances force you to change and release parts of yourself that you have outgrown. While letting go can be extremely painful, the eighth house views this type of death as cleansing and regenerative, a necessary part of your expansion and growth. Importantly, entering an eighth house year does not mean you'll face your own death. More often, it is about the transformation that occurs through letting go and allowing aspects of yourself or your life to fall away and die.

Clare Martin, author of *Mapping the Psyche*, emphasizes the importance of knocking carefully before entering the eighth house, as the topics here are often deeply buried. These matters are often tied to previous relationships, childhood wounds or your ancestors.

Entering your Eighth House year

Overview

ENTERING YOUR EIGHTH house year signifies a period of profound transformation. This often occurs through the process of letting go, allowing aspects of yourself or your life that are no longer serving you to fall away and die. This symbolic death paves the way for personal growth and renewal.

While it may feel like an intense year and issues around grief and loss may surface, these challenges present opportunities for significant emotional clearing.

The eighth house is also associated with debt, making this an opportune time to examine what you owe and to whom. This period encourages you to take proactive steps in addressing and clearing your debts, thereby freeing yourself from financial and emotional indebtedness to others. This can lead to a greater sense of liberation and self-empowerment.

Embracing change and surrendering to the mysteries of life can be a helpful incantation during your eighth house year. By acknowledging and working through deep-seated issues, you can emerge from your eighth house year with a renewed sense of clarity and purpose.

House support

Self-reflection: This is a powerful year to reflect on intimacy and how you experienced it within your past relationships. It is likely that these encounters will have shaped your behaviors in current relationships so be aware of how comfortable you are allowing other people to get close to you. If you are noticing repeating patterns and triggers, this is a potent year to work with a therapist to explore these beliefs more deeply.

Healing rituals: As ancestral stories can strongly influence your eighth house environment, engaging with ancestral healing work such as family constellations can heal these ancient stories, even when the personal circumstances aren't clear. As the lines of separation are thinner this year, notice if the energy of one of your ancestors feels closer.

Dying well: Stephen Jenkinson is the author of *Die Wise* – he has worked alongside dying people for over 20 years and he talks about how living well encompasses dying well. His book is a guide to the many faces of death and looks at how attitudes have changed over time and it's possible to see your death as an opportunity for great grace and power.

Eighth House

Journal prompts

What cultural or spiritual beliefs do I hold about death, and how do they influence my perspective on life?

How do I perceive the current level of intimacy in my relationships?

How do I feel about my connection to my ancestors and their unresolved issues? What can I do to honour and heal those legacies?

How do I feel about the concept of intimacy?

How do I envision my own death, and what feelings arise when I think about it?

A Eighth House Activity
Writing your own eulogy

This exercise allows you to reflect deeply on your life's journey and the legacy you wish to leave behind. By writing your own eulogy, you can gain clarity on your values, goals and the impact you want to have on the world.

Time: 1 hour
Tools: Paper, pens.

1. Prepare your space
* Find a warm and comfortable place where you won't be disturbed.

2. Visualize your funeral
* Picture your funeral and imagine your perfect setting, one that reflects the life you have lived. Try to do this without letting emotions overwhelm you.

3. Envision your passing
* Think about your ideal passing, including the age at which you transition and the circumstances of your death.
* Reflect on how you wish to bid farewell to this world.

4. Consider your legacy
* Contemplate how you aspire to be remembered by those whose lives you've touched.

5. Write your eulogy
* Take this opportunity to write a narrative of your life, including the years ahead and what you would like to achieve and be recognized for.
* Let your imagination roam freely as you contemplate the imprint you wish to leave on the world.

6. Preserve your eulogy
* Once you have written your eulogy, keep it in a safe place. You can revisit it the next time you enter the eighth house, 12 years from now.

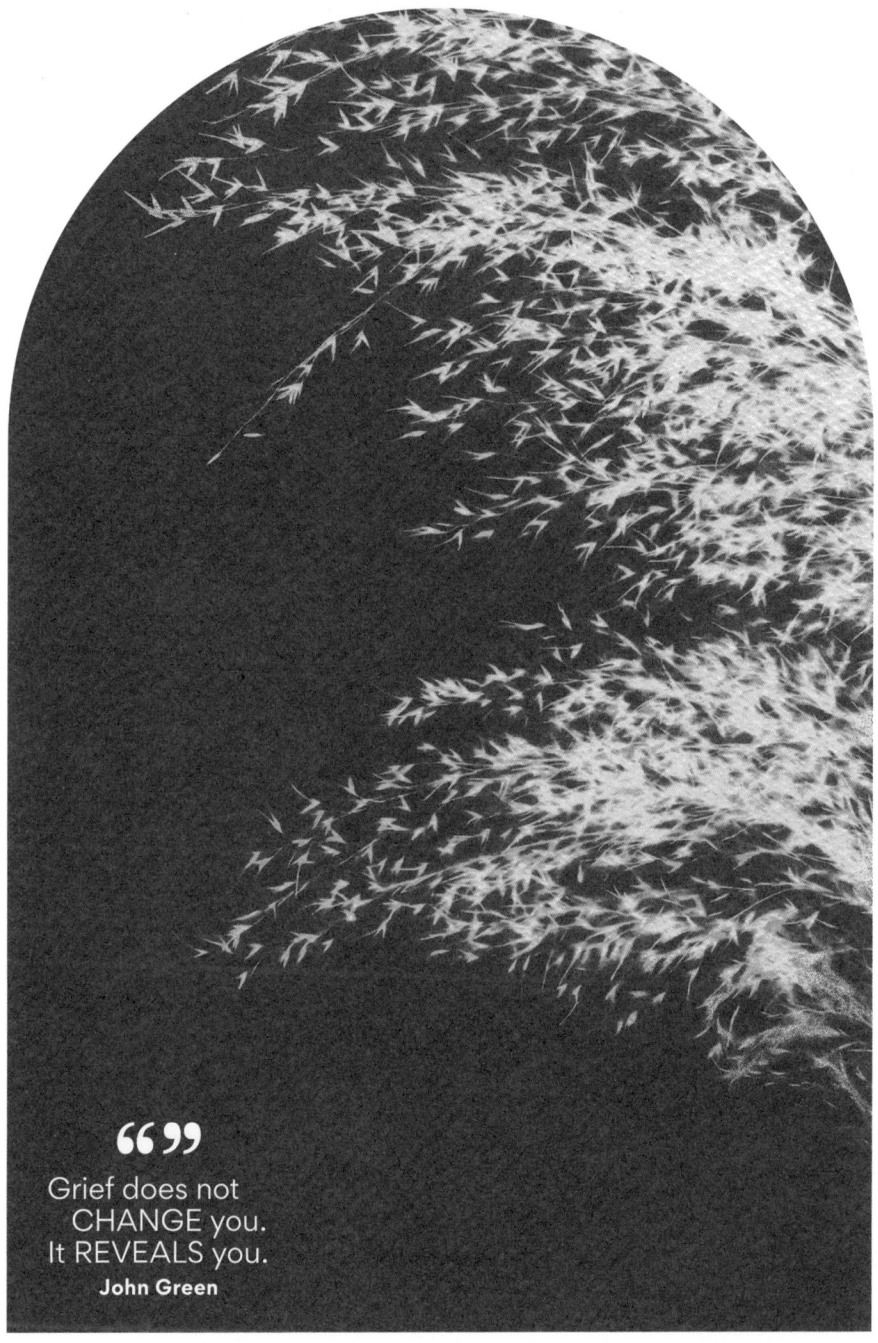

66 99

Grief does not
CHANGE you.
It REVEALS you.
John Green

A Eighth House Meditation
Clearing ancestral love wounds

Follow the basic relaxation meditation on page 12.

Crystal: Labradorite
Essential oil: Ylang ylang

As you stand inside the large wheel presenting your natal chart you are drawn to the eighth house door and immediately notice the rich texture of the door. You walk over to it and your guide, the lord of the eighth house appears next to you and passes you a large wooden key. You slowly turn the key and push the heavy door open. You find yourself in a long dark tunnel lit with candles. As the door closes behind you, you follow in your guide's footsteps, finding yourself going deeper into the tunnel of darkness.

You emerge from the tunnel to find yourself standing in a clearing under the night sky. Though the sky is dark, the moon illuminates the landscape, revealing an ancient well situated in front of you. You touch the cold stones and peer in, looking down at the depths of the water beneath you. You see the moon's reflection in the water, and just as you recognize your face reflected in the clear water, it changes to the face of someone else. Your guide tells you that this is your ancestor wishing to connect with you, to help heal an issue you both share.

You see a wooden handle to your right that connects to a rope and a beautiful pail on the ground next to the well. You pick the pail up and gently lower the rope into the water, letting the bucket collect water before pulling it back towards you. You are drawn to drink this water and as you take your first sip, you close your eyes and feel a tingling sensation throughout your body.

As you open your eyes you see a figure standing next to your guide. The face that you just saw in the water is now opposite you and you meet their eyes as you stand in front of each other. Your ancestor smiles and tells you who they are and how they are related to you.

They share that you both have a similar block around the flow of intimacy, and as they started this story, they wish to be the ones to complete it. They tell you about their life and how love was thwarted for them through circumstances beyond their control, setting in motion a block and a hardening around love and deep soul connections that still affect you.

They say that this is the time to stop. They place their hand over your heart and you feel great heat. As they take their hand away, you notice a hard black rock in their hand that was over your heart – they tell you this was trapped in your heart and that you carried it out of misplaced family loyalty.

As your ancestor leaves, they place this rock in your hand and tell you to release it in your own way.

You peer once again into the deep waters of the well. You hold the rock for the last time, thanking it for connecting you to your ancestors, but acknowledging it is now time to let it go. You realize that you can connect with your ancestors through pleasure rather than pain.

You drop the rock into the water and hear it splash as it reaches the bottom.

You notice that you feel lighter throughout your body. Your heart feels more open, more expansive. Ready to allow people in to see all of you.

Your guide tells you it's time. You follow them back into the tunnel, through the darkness, back to the eighth house portal door. You pull the large wooden door towards you and step out of the eighth house, back into your life.

66 99

The moment of surrender is not when life is OVER. It's when it BEGINS.
Marianne Williamson

The Ninth House

Ages

8 | 20 | 32 | 44 | 56 | 68 | 80 | 92

Keywords

Faith, higher education,
long distance travel

Element

Fire

Mantra

I trust in the guidance of the universe
and find meaning in every experience.

The Ninth House environment

THE NINTH HOUSE, traditionally called the House of God, is where themes connected to beliefs, faith and philosophy are placed. While the collective relationship to religion has changed significantly since Hellenistic times, this house continues to represent the spiritual dimensions where you are likely to ask the big questions of life.

This house examines what underpins you and how that foundation enables you to find meaning and purpose within the broad spectrum of your life. As a fire house, identity and freedom are intrinsically linked to this placement, often experienced as a call to action. Within this house lies a strong drive to broaden your horizons and gain knowledge from a wide variety of sources.

One way people seek greater wisdom is through higher education. Unlike the third house, which focuses on the concrete mind and everyday facts that don't require you to think outside the box, the ninth house is more interested in the higher or abstract mind. Howard Sasportas explains in *The Twelve Houses* that these journeys of the mind are about finding underlying meaning and significance in events, feeding into your philosophy of life, and helping you understand your connection to the bigger picture.

Long distance travel is also a strong element belonging to the ninth house as it is often only through leaving the familiarity of everyday life that a new perspective can emerge where you are able to see your own beliefs more clearly.

As spirituality and 'God' is part of the ninth house; some people experience this quest for meaning as more personal and private. This could take the form of reflection and contemplation as you search for deeper meaning through service and worship.

Ultimately the underlying notion of the ninth house is about seeking a greater meaning and purpose. This house is about what happens when you take yourself away from everyday distractions and are able to have a clearer view of what is truly meaningful to you and how that supports your experience of life.

66 99

The two most important days in life are the day you are BORN and the day you find out WHY.
Mark Twain

Entering your Ninth House year

Overview

ENTERING YOUR NINTH HOUSE year is a time to reflect on the big questions of life. The more you can step back and observe your life, the more you will gain. For some, there may be an undeniable call to get their passport out and broaden their horizons through travel. However, you can also gain great wisdom from different cultures without leaving home.

Reflecting on the last time you visited the ninth house is incredibly useful. As this year is about expanding your vision of life, paying attention to emerging themes can provide valuable insights. Consider the patterns, challenges and growth experiences from that time and how they can inform your current journey.

At times, you may feel a void or sense of emptiness. This can be a powerful starting point. Your journey this year is about finding meaning that makes life worth living. Embrace this opportunity to explore new philosophies, spiritual practices and educational pursuits as these are likely to resonate more strongly this year.

Your quest for meaning may lead you to question long-held beliefs. Be open to this process, as it is a natural part of the ninth house year.

House support

Take a course: This is an ideal year to pro-actively expand your mind. What is it that inspires and expands your views on life? While you may wish to revisit education more formally through a college or university, you may also wish to chart your own educational route and immerse yourself in a new topic through research and your own personal study.

Travel: Of all the astrological years, this is the one where the quest to find the meaning of life is at its peak. While this house is associated with long distance travel, it is not necessarily the miles that you travel but the distance that you are able to create away from your everyday life. The purpose of ninth house travel is about creating an adventure which will enable you to view yourself and your life differently, so pay attention if you are drawn to a particular country or culture at this time.

Write a book: If you have been thinking about writing a book then this is a great year to start. The ninth house is connected to the world of publishing, reaching large audiences through the written word, sharing your thoughts and insights.

Ninth House

Journal prompts

What are my beliefs about God or a higher power? How have these beliefs shaped my life?

What travel experiences have broadened my perspective? Where do I feel called to visit next?

What personal experiences have challenged my beliefs? How have they contributed to my growth?

What questions do I have about the meaning of life?

What inspires my sense of adventure and curiosity?

A Ninth House Activity
The jigsaw of life

By visually mapping out your foundations, current life and spiritual connection, this exercise helps you identify areas for growth and focus during your ninth house year.

Time: 30 minutes
Tools: A4 paper, colouring pencils, pencil, scissors.

1. Prepare your paper
* Divide your piece of paper (landscape orientation) into three horizontal sections, drawing the lines with your pencil.
* Within each horizontal section, divide the area into four boxes, making a total of 12 boxes.

2. Bottom section – foundations
* This section represents your foundations – what underpins you. Write down any memories, beliefs, past relationships, schooling and anything else that makes you who you are.

3. Middle section – present life
* This section presents your life at this current time. Think of all the aspects of your life and include them here, such as family, partners, pets, work and hobbies.

4. Top section – faith and connection
* This section is about faith and your connection to something bigger than yourself. Reflect on what comes forward and how it wants to be included.

5. Bring your sections to life
* Use words and/or images to vividly illustrate each box.

6. Create a jigsaw puzzle
* Once you have completed each of the 12 boxes, use scissors to cut around each box, creating a total of 12 separate jigsaw pieces.

7. Identify the gaps
* Close your eyes so that you are unable to see the jigsaw pieces and remove four pieces.
* Now place your jigsaw back together and notice where the gaps are.
* Reflect on which sections are missing in your picture of life.

8. Reflect and enhance

* Can you relate to these being gaps in your life?
* Consider how you can focus on enhancing these areas of your life during your ninth house year.

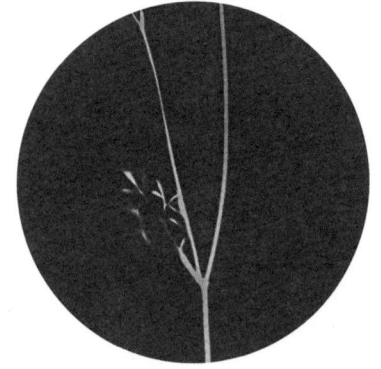

" "

I want to live with an
AWARENESS and
APPRECIATION of all
the layers...
Julia Alvarez

A Ninth House Meditation

Expanding your horizons

Follow the basic relaxation meditation on page 12.

Crystal: Lapis lazuli
Essential oil: Myrrh

As you stand inside your natal chart you see all the 12 doors surrounding you. You walk towards door number nine and take a moment to focus on the number positioned in the middle of the door. As you stare at it, the number starts to shimmer and at this point the door opens. You step forward, crossing over the portal into the ninth house. You find yourself in a familiar safe place in nature. This is a place that you have visited in person or in your dreams.

The night is dark, and in the distance you see a fire burning with figures sitting around it. In front of you is a lantern with a candle burning brightly. You pick up the lantern and start to walk towards the fire. As you get closer, you hear the voices and discussions taking place around this fire. The nine figures around the fire look up and start to clap, happy to see you. One figure gets up and leaves the circle; you are warmly embraced and this figure tells you that they are your guide of the ninth house.

Your guide explains that this is a group of wise elders from different cultures, religions and decades, bonded together in support of you. They meet every 12 years when you enter your ninth house year, and their mission is to help you see life differently and expand your mind by planting seeds in your life.

Take a moment to look at these figures – how do you feel when you see them?

Your guide asks you to sit down next to them, and you feel the warmth of the fire. Next to where you are sitting, you see a large book that your guide encourages you to pick up and open. In front of you is a large empty page. However, within moments, this page flickers to life, and you see an image of yourself in your day-to-day life, going through habitual and familiar routines.

You then see flashes of your day with your guide standing close by.

Your guide explains that while their presence is invisible to you, they are working hard to stay connected to you. You start to see acts that you once thought were meaningless as meaningful – books that grabbed your attention, songs on the radio, the conversations of strangers. Your guide informs you that these are all seeds planted to help you understand that you are part of something much bigger.

Your guide tells you to turn to the next page, and again you see an empty piece of paper. Before long, this page comes alive, and you see yourself in your life when you are feeling connected to the ninth house energy. You notice a palpable excitement, a sense of adventure, as you see that you are living your life as a quest, a search for meaning.

You continue to watch and see yourself overcoming obstacles with newfound wisdom, connecting deeply with others and exploring new horizons with curiosity and courage. The image shifts to show moments of joy and fulfilment, where your actions are aligned with your higher purpose.

Your guide then asks you to reflect on these images and the feelings they evoke. They encourage you to carry this sense of adventure and connection back into your daily life, reminding you that the seeds of wisdom and inspiration planted during this time will continue to grow and flourish.

Before you return, your guide gives you a small, symbolic object. What do you receive? This object represents the knowledge and insights you've gained and serves as a reminder of your connection to the ninth house energy.

With a final embrace, your guide and the wise elders bid you farewell, their warmth and support lingering with you. You pick up your lantern and follow the path back to the place in nature. You find yourself outside the door, and again you push it open and step back over the portal. The ninth house door closes behind you, and you carry with you a renewed sense of purpose, adventure and connection to the greater meaning of your life.

The Tenth House

Ages

9 | 21 | 33 | 45 | 57 | 69 | 81 | 93

Keywords

Career, success, social status

Element

Earth

Mantra

My dedication and hard work lead to extraordinary achievements.

The Tenth House environment

POSITIONED AT THE TOP of the chart, the tenth house is the most visible of all the astrological houses. Traditionally this house used to be regarded as the house of marriage as in the Hellenistic times, marriage was the main route available for women to elevate their social standing and gain public respect. However, as most women nowadays lead independent lives, this connotation to marriage has fallen away and the tenth house is now regarded as the public face that both men and women put on when they are seeking recognition and success out in the world.

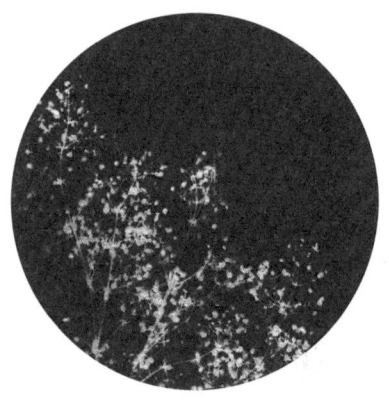

Strongly connected to your career and your career ambitions, this house is about the qualities and behaviours that you hold in esteem and wish to be associated with. Unlike the sixth house which is about the day-to-day work required to pay the bills and put food on the table; the tenth house is about your inner vocation, the work that you feel your soul is called to do. While your desired income may be included here, generally achieving success in this house is more about how you take your place in the world rather than being purely motivated by monetary gain.

This house is also symbolic of authority, both your own leadership as well as those people perceived to be in authority to you, such as an employer. As this placement is opposite the fourth house, which is historically connected to the less visible role of the father, the tenth house illustrates the parent or caregiver who was most dominant or visible in your life.

Howard Sasportas in *The Twelve Houses* quotes from Liz Greene when he describes the tenth house as being your 'social shorthand'. Ultimately this house is about how you would most like to be seen by others, the best version of yourself.

Entering your Tenth House year

Overview

THIS IS A PARTICULARLY powerful year as the tenth house (along with the first, fourth and seventh) is seen as one of the most potent houses. Entering your tenth house year means that you are entering a time of higher visibility as you have the opportunity to elevate your reputation, status and career.

As your career is directly under the celestial spotlight there will be a natural focus on your work ambitions and how you can attain greater success. This is a good time to consider what true success means to you so that you proactively step forward and utilize this tenth house energy.

You may also find that any issues that are hindering your career or public aspirations come into prominence as this is your year to resolve any shadows blocking your ability to flourish.

Finally, as the tenth house is also part of the parental axis, your parents, particularly your mother, may well have a stronger presence this year. It is useful to consider any of her unlived dreams to ensure that you are following your own path and staying true to your own authority rather than trying to, unconsciously, take her place in the world.

House support

Career mentor: As the focus this year is on the work that you feel called to do (rather than have to do), working with a mentor is especially useful. Often when something is of great importance, the fear to step forward and claim it can feel heightened so having an external pair of eyes to help you shine and gain greater recognition is to your advantage.

Enter for an award: The tenth house is the highest point in your chart and is often a point of culmination and reward after a great deal of hard work. This energy is primed for recognition so entering for an award or a form of recognition is a brilliant way to work with the tenth house.

Personal branding: Regardless of the type of work that you do, this is a powerful year to allow yourself to be seen so consider how you can illuminate your own public relations. You may wish to be more active on social media, offer your expertise within an area or create your own personal website or blog.

Tenth House

Journal prompts

In what ways do I strive for visibility and recognition in my work?

If I could design my perfect job, what would it look like and why?

What stories or beliefs about work and success do I need to release to follow my true calling?

What work activities make me lose track of time because I enjoy them so much?

How would my life change if I fully embraced and welcomed success?

A Tenth House Activity
This is your life

Find a partner to do this exercise with, for accountability and support. Reflect on and celebrate your life achievements, recognizing the influence of key people and envisioning future successes. Use a large red book as your narration tool to chronicle your life story.

Time: Ongoing
Tools: Large red notebook or journal.

1. Starting your story
* Family legacy: Start with the story of your grandparents and parents, acknowledging their roles and impact on your life. Write or discuss significant events, values and lessons learned from them.
* Early life: Continue your story in chronological order. Include memories from your childhood, school years and higher education. Reflect on key moments that shaped you.

2. Career and milestones
* First job and beyond: Document your career journey, including your first job, major career changes and professional achievements. Highlight moments of growth, challenges overcome and successes.
* Personal achievements: Include significant personal milestones such as relationships, hobbies and passions that have enriched your life.

3. Inviting guests
* Imagine who would be invited onto your 'This is Your Life' TV show. Consider family members, friends, mentors and anyone who has played a pivotal role in your journey.
* Guest contributions: Reflect on what each person would say about you. What stories and experiences would they share? How did they influence your path?

4. Sharing in pairs
* Take turns sharing different pages of your book with your partner.
* Discussion points: Explain the role of each person mentioned

in your book and how they influenced your development. Discuss what you are most proud of in your life.

and future aspirations. Share any final thoughts or commitments to action with your partner.

5. Envisioning the future

* Fast forward 12 years to your next visit to the tenth house. Imagine what achievements and successes you would like to include in your future story.
* Goal setting: Write down or discuss your future aspirations, both personal and professional. Consider the steps needed to achieve these goals.

6. Reflection

* Reflect on the entire exercise. How has recounting your life story and envisioning your future impacted your perspective on success and fulfilment?
* Takeaways: Identify key insights and lessons learned from this activity. How can you apply these insights to your current and future endeavours?
* Conclude the activity by summarizing your reflections

66 99

Let yourself be
SILENTLY drawn by
the strange pull of
what you really LOVE.
Rumi

A Tenth House Meditation
Celebrating achievements

Follow the basic relaxation meditation on page 12.

Crystal: Black tourmaline
Essential oil: Clary sage

As you stand inside the large wheel of your natal chart you take a moment to look at the 12 doors surrounding you. You turn around to face the tenth house door and walk towards it. You notice this is the largest of all the doors and it seems to loom boldly in front of you. You turn the handle and the door immediately opens.

You step over the tenth house portal and find yourself in a large noisy banquet hall. There is a long table filled with food and around the table are a number of guests, talking, laughing and making merry. You see many people that have at some point been part of your life. Even the people that you don't recognize seem familiar in some way. One of the guests spots you and roars with excitement. Everyone follows their gaze and there is a universal eruption of delight.

An older figure comes and immediately greets you with a warm embrace. This figure leads you to the top of the table and you sit in an elevated chair. The older figure says that the feast is in honour of you. This is a celebration of what you have achieved in your past 12 years and this group comes together every time you enter a tenth house year.

A drink is placed in your hand and all the people sitting at the table raise a toast to you. Then each guest, starting from your left, stands up and says a quality that they wish to acknowledge in you. When each guest has spoken, a silence claims the room. No one eats, drinks or talks.

Then the older figure stands up and in front of you holds a key on a long chain. What does this key look like? The figure tells you that this key will unlock a trunk that holds a key ingredient of your current tenth house year. You take the key, which feels cold in your hand and see a trunk by your side. You turn the key in the lock and slowly lift the trunk lid.

You see a large piece of glimmering black tourmaline, which you pick up. The dark crystal's energy pulsates in your hand. You notice letters etched deeply within the crystal spelling the word 'speden'. The older figure says that this is the old English word for success; that this signifies a year of triumph ahead.

The cheers from your fellow guests erupt once more and you notice music fills the room. The celebration of you commences.

The older figure says that it is time to go and explains that the party will reconvene in 12 years when you next enter the tenth house year. The figure walks you out of the tenth house portal. The guests cheer as you walk away and then you hear silence as the door closes behind you.

66 99

Life is a GRAND CELEBRATION, every moment an opportunity to dance
Osho

The Eleventh House

Ages

10 | 22 | 34 | 46 | 58 | 70 | 82 | 94

Keywords

Friends, groups, long-term hopes and wishes

Element

Air

Mantra

My friendships and alliances support my growth and bring me closer to achieving my dreams.

The Eleventh House environment

☽ ● ☾

THE ELEVENTH HOUSE is about your tribe. This is the placement where you will find your non-blood family, the people who you choose to share your time with as they on some level align with your ideals and outlook on life. Unlike the seventh house which is about one-on-one relationships, the eleventh house is about one-to-many relationships which is typically symbolized through friendships. However, this also includes all groups where people share a similar (often unrealized) vision or aspiration such as unions, charities, political parties, memberships or societies.

Traditionally the eleventh house was called the house of hopes and wishes. While this seems unrelated to the notion of groups, the underlying context is about the human wish to be more than they are and how this can be achieved by connecting to something bigger than themselves such as a friendship circle or a social network.

This house remains connected to the concept of hopes and wishes, however, nowadays it is premised by 'long-term hopes and wishes', as this house is future facing and is looking at what it is that you wish to achieve.

❝❞

Alone we can do so LITTLE; together we can do so MUCH.

Helen Keller

Opposite the fifth house of pleasure, the eleventh house is also about self-expression. However, unlike the fifth house which is more focused on expressing your own pleasures and desires; the eleventh house is about how you are able to express yourself within the confines of a group. Rather than experiencing this as repressive, the intention is more about how you adapt your behaviour in alignment with the needs and identity of the group.

Ultimately the eleventh house is about the call to find your clan. Unlike family members (third house) or parents (fourth and tenth house), this is about who you choose as your allies. Typically in the eleventh house there is a common thread of working together for a shared dream which is often about the betterment of humanity.

Entering your Eleventh House year

Overview

WHEN YOU ENTER your eleventh house year, community, tribe and future dreams are all under the spotlight. It is likely that you will experience an element of change in these areas; friendships may fall away so that new ones can emerge and your allegiance and sense of belonging to specific groups or communities may radically alter.

Rather than holding on to the past or taking any of these changes personally, it is more beneficial for you to understand that these shifts are an important part of your evolution. As this house is connected to your long-term hopes and wishes, you may find that your future plans also change and what was once important, no longer has the same sway.

As an air house, the focus is on people and ideas so this is a great year to evaluate your thoughts and ensure that your future hopes and wishes are in alignment with the person that you are now, rather than the person you once were.

Engaging with diverse groups of people is also particularly helpful during this year as different mindsets will bring forward new possibilities and aspirations that you may not have previously considered.

House support

Join a new group: This is a great year for socializing and meeting new people. While the seventh house is about committed relationships, the eleventh house connections are less intense and more about sharing ideas. Notice what topics you are particularly interested in at this time and seek out ways to meet people who share this common interest.

Expand your network: This is a powerful year for alliances so directing this energy into expanding your network is a great use of your eleventh house year. Ultimately this is about new people, new ideas and new insights which will ultimately move you closer to your long-term hopes and wishes.

Sow seeds for the future: As the house of long-term dreams, the energy is ripe for sowing seeds for the future. Focus your mind on what it is that you would like to achieve and think about how you could connect with others to make that happen. Write down your intentions and create your own New Moon ritual – the Aquarius New Moon in February is particularly potent.

Eleventh House

Journal prompts

What qualities do I seek in the friendships and groups I choose to be a part of?

What fears come to mind when I think about expressing myself within a group setting?

What role do I typically play within my social circles and groups?

What have I learned from my past experiences in groups or teams?

How do my long-term hopes and dreams inspire and motivate me in my daily life?

A Eleventh House Activity
Your vision board

Of all the years, the eleventh house year is perfect for creating a vision board. As the home to your long-term hopes and wishes, this is an ideal time to look to the future and think about what you wish to accomplish.

Imagine this vision board represents the next 12 years of your life. Reflect on what is important to you right now and what you wish to achieve in the long run.

Time: 1–2 hours
Tools: Large piece of paper, scissors, glue, a variety of magazines.

1. Intuitive selection
* Flip through the magazines and allow yourself to intuitively choose images and words that resonate with you.
* Consider aspects of your life such as career, relationships, personal growth, health and contributions to society.

2. Create your vision board
* Once you have gathered a substantial pile of images and words, start arranging them on your piece of paper.
* Glue them down in a way that feels meaningful and inspiring to you.

3. Reflect and set intentions
* Take time to reflect on your vision board. What themes emerge? How do these images and words align with your long-term hopes and dreams?
* Set clear intentions for the next 12 years, using your vision board as a guiding tool.

Place your vision board somewhere you can see it regularly. Let it serve as a reminder of your goals and aspirations, inspiring you to take steps towards realizing your dreams every day.

A Eleventh House Meditation
A reconnection to your soul tribe

Follow the basic relaxation meditation on page 12.

Crystal: Celestite
Essential oil: Sandalwood

As you stand inside the large circle of your natal chart, you immediately see the eleventh house door before you. You walk up to it and stand outside. There is no handle on the door, so you knock gently and it is opened by a figure dressed in white. The figure introduces themselves as your guide, the lord of your eleventh house and they invite you on a journey.

You immediately feel at ease with your guide and follow them along a wide corridor with large windows on each side. As you walk alongside your guide, you notice an almost invisible thread connecting you to them. Your guide notices your curiosity and explains that while everyone is energetically connected, there are specific people who are part of your soul tribe and with them, there is a cord of light that connects you.

At the end of the corridor, you find a huge staircase. Some stairs lead downward, and others lead upward. Your guide takes the upward stairs, and you follow in their footsteps. At the top of the stairs, you look out of the window and notice how high up you are, how far the ground appears from this position.

Your guide leads you into a room where you see a circle of 12 chairs positioned around one chair in the middle. Your guide suggests you sit in the middle chair. You take your place and close your eyes. Although the chairs are empty, you sense the energy of people, of souls, connected to each chair. Your guide tells you that you are sensing the presence of your soul tribe. While they are out in the world, you remain connected, and as your guide speaks, you sense silver threads of light connecting each one of you.

Your guide explains that while you all have different missions and aspirations in this lifetime, when your paths cross, your cells register their presence, and there is an unconscious call to help and support your fellow soul tribe. Even though the threads of light are invisible in your everyday life, your tribe has its own unique energy, and on an unconscious level, you are in tune with the emotional wellbeing of your tribe, feeling each of their highs and lows.

With your eyes still closed, you hear voices talking. Your guide tells you that you are listening to a memory of the last time your tribe sat in the circle together. This was the time before you were all born, when each soul discussed their mission for rebirth. You notice they call you by a different name, and your guide tells you this is your 'soul name'.

You feel a sense of complete belonging, acceptance and love.

You are aware that you don't want to leave this energy, this circle. Your guide tells you that there is more to do, your light is still required, but when the time is right, your soul group will come back together to reconnect and regroup.

Slowly, you stand up and leave the circle. You follow your guide back to the stairs, along the long corridor with windows on each side, back to the eleventh house door. Your guide says they look forward to seeing you in 12 years when you return to the eleventh house.

You step through the eleventh house portal and the door slowly closes behind you.

> **66 99**
>
> Find a GROUP of people who CHALLENGE and INSPIRE you, spend a lot of time with them, and it will change your life.
>
> **Amy Poehler**

The Twelfth House

Ages

11 | 23 | 35 | 47 | 59 | 71 | 83 | 95

Keywords

Unconscious, retreat, healing

Element

Water

Mantra

As I complete this transformative 12-year cycle, I release old patterns and welcome profound spiritual healing and renewal.

The Twelfth House environment

HISTORICALLY, THE TWELFTH house wasn't the most welcoming of houses. Dana Gerhardt, in her essay on astrological houses, states that this house was traditionally referred to as 'the valley of miseries,' 'the dark den of sorrow and horror', 'the portal of toil', and the house of 'Bad Spirit'. Due to its weak positional placement, it was believed that all activities found here could only detract from your life, as this was considered the dwelling place of hidden enemies, self-undoing, sickness and suffering.

However, modern astrology takes a more balanced view, asserting that there are no inherently bad houses. The twelfth house, as a water house along with the fourth and eighth houses, connects to the more introverted and invisible areas of your life. Rhetorius, a seventh century astrologer, described the twelfth house as being 'in-between worlds', a notion that still holds strong. Today, rather than being viewed as a confinement of doom and misery, this house is seen as a doorway to vast oceans of spiritual wisdom and support.

The veil separating the material and spiritual realms is at its thinnest when the twelfth house is activated. Behaviours, choices and attitudes are often influenced by your unconscious inheritance. Known as the house of the womb and family karma, unresolved stories from your parents and ancestors are entwined with this house, indicating that issues arising here are likely seeded by your lineage.

The theme of the hidden runs deep in the twelfth house as this is also regarded as the house of institutions, monasteries, nunneries, hospitals and prisons – all the places where the invisible members of society are placed.

While the twelfth house can initially feel confusing and unclear, it is helpful to remember that this is the most psychic of all houses. The boundaries here are the most fluid, and through this porous filter, you can access collective wisdom and sacred knowledge. When used well, this knowledge can open your life to previously unseen possibilities.

Entering your Twelfth House year

Overview

WHEN YOU ENTER your twelfth house year, you are completing a 12-year cycle, marking the final stage of a long journey. Intuitively, there is a call to completion as aspects of yourself and your life come to a close. Self-reflection becomes more important, making it beneficial to review the past 12 years and decide what you wish to carry forward into the next cycle.

This year may feel quieter, with the energy turning inward. You are likely to feel more sensitive and may find that you have less motivation for external pursuits. Traditionally known as the house of sickness, this doesn't imply you will become unwell, but it can mean that your vitality levels might be lower. Social interactions may become more draining, prompting a need for more sleep, rest and emotional and physical retreat.

During this year, your intuition will be heightened. Given the association of the twelfth house with self-undoing, it is important to remain vigilant about your blind spots. Proactively identify behaviours that block your spiritual growth and pay attention to signs from the unseen world. Journaling and meditation can be particularly useful tools, helping you access deeper wisdom and clarity.

House support

Retreat: Getting distance from your everyday life can be particularly helpful in a twelfth house year as there is a yearning for space and time alone. It is often during a twelfth house year that people are drawn to retreats. If taking a week or weekend 'out' isn't possible, then scheduling pockets of 'you time' with a clear intention to switch off from technology and the usual stimulus of life can work well.

Family constellations: Ancestral wounds when rejected can repeat through different generations. As the twelfth house is aligned to unresolved stories from the past, you might be drawn to attend to this part of life during this time. Family constellation is a modality that opens the door to the healing of inherited family patterns to ensure that the past does not block your future.

Floatation tank: A floatation tank is a cocoon of water filled with dead sea salts. As the temperature of the water matches your body, when you float there is a sense of expansion as the boundaries of where you end and the water starts are eroded.

Twelfth House

Journal prompts

What behaviours or habits do I suspect are undermining my spiritual growth?

What hidden aspects of myself am I afraid to confront? Why do they intimidate me?

How do I feel about spending more time in solitude? What emotions does it evoke?

What unresolved stories from my past or family history do I need to address, how do they affect my present life?

What messages or signs from the unseen world have I noticed? How can I interpret them to guide my spiritual journey?

A Twelfth House Activity
Creating your twelfth house map

Time: 1 hour
Tools: A5 or A4 size paper for drawing and writing, set of colouring pencils, incense, calming music.

1. Create a peaceful space
* Find a quiet place where you won't be disturbed. This could be a cosy corner of your home, a quiet room or any place where you feel safe and relaxed.
* Turn off your phone or set it to silent to ensure you have uninterrupted time for this activity.

2. Enhance your environment
* Play any music that brings you a sense of peace and calm. Music can help you get into a meditative and creative state of mind.
* Light some incense to create a serene and calming atmosphere.

3. Ground yourself
* Sit comfortably and close your eyes. Take a few deep breaths, inhaling deeply and exhaling slowly. Allow yourself to relax and become fully present in the moment.
* Listen to the music and feel its calming effects. Wait until you feel grounded and centred before you start.

4. Begin your map
* Take your paper and write at the top, 'My Twelfth House Map'.
* Draw an image of yourself in the centre of the paper. This can be a simple stick figure, a detailed self-portrait or any representation that feels right to you.

5. Add elements to your map
* Start by noticing what images, symbols or words you feel drawn to place next to your self-image.
* Ask yourself, 'What will I find in my twelfth house?' and allow your intuition to guide you. This could include dreams, fears, hidden talents, spiritual guides or anything else that feels relevant.
* Embrace your imagination and creativity. There is no need to censor yourself –

allow whatever comes up to be expressed on the paper.

6. Trust your intuition
* As you draw and write, trust that your intuition is guiding you to include elements that are significant for your twelfth house year.
* Include symbols, images or words that feel important, even if you don't fully understand their meaning right now. Your subconscious mind knows what needs to be on the map.

7. Reflect on your map
* Once you have completed your map, take a few moments to look at it. Notice any patterns, themes or insights that emerge.
* Reflect on how these elements might relate to your inner world, your spiritual journey and your personal growth.

8. Use your map as a guide
* Keep your twelfth house map in a place where you can see it regularly. Use it as a tool for reflection and guidance throughout your year.
* Revisit your map periodically to see if new insights or additions come to mind. This map can evolve as you do.

❝❞

Don't let the NOISE of others' opinions DROWN out your own inner voice.
Steve Jobs

A Twelfth House Meditation
The bridge of eternal connections

Follow the basic relaxation meditation on page 12.

Crystal: Siberian fir
Essential oil: Moonstone

You are about to embark on an exploration within your twelfth house. Begin by imagining yourself entering your natal chart. Picture walking into a giant circle, surrounded by 12 doors, each numbered and leading to one of your astrological houses. Your destination is the door with the number 12.

Take a moment to observe this door. What does it look like? You realize the door is locked. As you stand before it, a familiar figure appears next to you – your guide, the overseer of your twelfth house.

Your guide explains that the twelfth house can be easy to get lost in, but you will navigate it using your third eye, the powerful point between your eyebrows where you access your intuition. Your guide places a hand over your third eye and you feel a deep sense of warmth and light. They tell you that your third eye is now activated.

Your guide hands you a key to unlock the door. Take note of the key's appearance. It is ornate and shimmering, almost magical. Your guide reassures you that while you will travel through this house alone, each step is protected and you can call on your spiritual support team at any time.

Before you proceed, your guide gives you a map. This is not an ordinary map – it glows with a faint light and shifts as if alive. Your guide tells you that this map will lead you to an important meeting on the bridge of eternal connections, but you must trust your intuition to interpret it. The landmarks on the map will reveal themselves as you move forward.

Unlock the door and step into your twelfth house. Allow yourself a moment to adjust to this new environment. What do you see? How do you feel?

Look at the map. It shows shifting symbols and paths. Trust your intuition to decipher the map's guidance. You notice a path forming on the map leading towards the bridge.

As you walk along the path, you feel a lightness and experience a sense of life that doesn't exist in your everyday world.

You see the bridge and notice a deep whirlpool of water beneath it. Observe the details of the bridge and the whirlpool. The bridge appears ancient and mystical, with intricate carvings and a soft glow. The whirlpool below seems powerful yet serene, swirling with energy.

On the other side, a figure emerges from the mists, walking towards you. This is one of your ancestors. Though you may not have met them in this lifetime, you feel a deep connection. Your ancestor is delighted to meet you in the middle of the bridge, where they tell you that you are carrying a burden that does not belong to you and that it must be released into the waters of time. What is it that you have been carrying?

By your feet, you see a bag containing this family burden passed down through generations. Pick up the bag, and when you are ready, drop it into the whirlpool below. Watch as it dissolves, spreading particles of light into the waters, which then calm. You immediately feel lighter.

Your ancestor tells you that it is time to leave, but you can return to the bridge whenever you wish, and the action you took will continue to ripple forward. Watch your ancestor return to the mists on the other side of the bridge.

Follow your route back to the twelfth house door, guided by the map which now shows the way clearly. Step back into your natal chart, hearing the door lock behind you. Your guide is waiting for you and congratulates you on your exploration. They assure you that your third eye will remain activated throughout your twelfth house year.

About Prue

Prue Nichols combines energetic healing, spiritual guidance and sacred astrology to transform everyday life. She has worked in the holistic field for over 20 years, creating treatments that alleviate pain and release emotional suffering.

www.pruenichols.com
Instagram @prue_nichols

Further reading

Brennan, Chris. (2017)
Hellenistic Astrology.
Amor Fati Publications

Chapman, Gary (2024)
The 5 Love Languages.
Northfield Publishing

Jenkinson, Stephen (2016)
Die Wise.
North Atlantic Books

Martin, Clare (2016)
Mapping the Psyche.
The Wessex Astrologer Ltd

Sasportas, Howard (2009)
The Twelve Houses.
LSA/Flare

Tompkins, Sue (2009)
The Contemporary Astrologer's Handbook.
LSA/Flare

First published:
Inner Work Project, 2024

Text copyright ©
Prue Nichols 2024
All rights reserved.

ISBN 978-1-916563-04-9

Graphic Design:
Supafrank

Printed in the UK by Pureprint

Further inspiration

The Inner Work Project is devoted to sharing ways in which we can all make the inner journey of discovery to meet our kindest, wisest selves; to heal and grow; to stop holding ourselves back, feel alive and nourished and purposeful.

Explore our titles:

www.innerworkproject.com
Instagram @innerworkproject